TRIUMPH AND TRIBULATION

H. W. TILMAN

Mountains and glaciers beyond Ny Alesund, Spitzbergen

TRIUMPH AND TRIBULATION

H. W. TILMAN

TILMAN

First published 1977 by Nautical Publishing Company
This edition published 2017 by Tilman Books
www.tilmanbooks.com
a joint venture by
Lodestar Books www.lodestarbooks.com
and Vertebrate Publishing www.v-publishing.co.uk

Cover design by Jane Beagley
Vertebrate Graphics Ltd. www.v-graphics.co.uk

Lodestar Books has asserted their right
to be identified as the Editor of this Work

Series editor Dick Wynne
Series researcher Bob Comlay

A CIP catalogue record for this book
is available from the British Library

ISBN 978-1-909461-42-0

Typeset in Baskerville from Storm Type Foundry
Printed and bound by Pulsio Print, Bulgaria
All papers used by Tilman Books are sourced responsibly

Contents

Photographs

Maps

Foreword

Andrew Craig-Bennett

M Y ONLY QUALIFICATION FOR WRITING THIS is that I crewed for HWT round Spitzbergen in 1974. I was lucky to hit a 'good crew year', with Paul Rheinsch, Alan Stockdale and David White, with the bonus of meeting Colin Putt, who had come down to Lymington to help with fitting out. I am not a climber, or even much of a walker and camper, so I can only comment on sailing and cookery.

I was unusual amongst HWT's crews only in that I had been taught to sail by my father, who had sailed since 1919, when he was sixteen, so I was used to sailing with a taciturn man in his seventies. We had not met before I joined the boat, in Lymington, on the day after my final exams. HWT struck me as smaller and more frail than I had pictured him; the frailty was illusory and vanished as soon as we were at sea. Contrary to his ascetic reputation, we went to the pub every evening after the day's work on the boat, and he was extremely good company. My enduring mental picture of him is in the pub, tweed jacketed, pipe and pint in hand.

HWT was a friend of Dr David Lewis, who had completed his circumnavigation of Antarctica in *Ice Bird* shortly before we set off—HWT's verdict was "That boat is too small for the weather there". He was also a friend of Mike McMullen, who very kindly gave us all a day out in the Solent on board his Newick trimaran *Three Cheers*—a boat as far removed from *Baroque* as one might imagine, even today. HWT was enthusiastic, and said that provided the boat was big enough to take the weight of stores and spares, he would like to try his sort of sailing in a fast trimaran.

Astern of us alongside the Berthon Boatyard was the Swan 65 *Sayula* which had just won the first Whitbread Round the World Race, and of course HWT was invited to dinner by David May of the Berthon to meet Ramon Carlin, her successful skipper and owner. "Very impressive" was his verdict.

I was interested in what one might term the technical aspects of small boat seamanship, as indeed I still am, so I watched how HWT went about things, with what I hope was informed interest. I may have gone so far as to badger HWT with questions, though he was far too courteous to discourage me. He had been at pains to learn the how to sail properly, and he learned the art of sailing heavy displacement gaff cutters, the type of boat then favoured for long voyages, from the most acknowledged experts, by crewing for Robert Somerset on *Iolaire*, by consulting Laurent Giles and Partners on what boat to buy for his purposes, by having Humphrey Barton and John Tew of that firm aboard *Mischief*, and latterly by seeking out and picking the brains of retired Bristol Channel pilots and westernmen.

It was Hum Barton, the brokerage partner in Laurent Giles and Partners, who sold him *Mischief* and who flew out to Portugal to give a hand on the delivery voyage back to Lymington. And why Lymington, where HWT kept his elderly gaff cutters at one of the grandest boatyards in Europe, the Berthon Boatyard? Because that was where Laurent Giles had his office.

It goes without saying that HWT was a thorough seaman. He was cautious, alert to all changes in the motion of the boat and to the weather and the seas, and a diligent and prudent navigator. He enjoyed, and was good at, all the marlinespike seamanship that goes with owning a large Victorian boat. I recall being on watch on the first occasion on our passage when conditions were, to my mind, starting to deteriorate. Towards the end of my watch, with Alan (my relief) stirring, I lashed the helm, looked around, and went below:

"Sir, I think it may be time to heave to."

"I'll come..."

"You're right. We'll take another reef down first."

So we did—an easy task with the big Appledore gear and its monstrous handle—made I think by Colin—and HWT proceeded to dig out a handy-billy and hook one block into the weather shrouds and the other into the clew of the reefed staysail. He brought the clew just to windward of the mast, then returned to the cockpit and lashed the helm half down. He spent quite a few minutes looking at how *Baroque* was doing, making small adjustments to the helm. She sat, heeling a little, making a square drift at about one knot, leaving a smooth to windward of the boat, with the luff of her mainsail lifting as she came up by a few degrees, and then filling as she bore off again. No water came on deck. We did not need fiddles on the saloon table. I was impressed.

HWT insisted on an anchor watch, even when alongside in port, and in fact we never broke our watches. At Ny-Alesund, I was ship-keeping on my own and I decided to end-for-end the Manila peak halyard, which was getting fat at one end and thin at the other, as natural fibre ropes will. When Paul and Alan came back aboard, Paul asked how many times I had been up and down the mast... HWT, knowing the trick, gave me the most tremendous wink... I had used the kedge warp as a lazy halyard, stitching the ends together, as my father had shown me.

HWT was very kind to the boat, and we sailed gently. Looking over the distances run and the time taken on passage I see that we averaged fifty miles a day, which is very gentle going (the 'standard figure' for any small yacht at that time was a hundred miles a day—today it will be more). He absolutely disliked running, and insisted on 'tacking downwind'. To make sure of this, he had a mainsheet that was decidedly short, and I concluded that he had had quite enough of the boom getting in the water, of gybes both regular and 'Imperial Chinese', and was going to take no chances with inexperienced helmsmen getting 'carried away'.

Indeed, about the most disabling accident that can come to pass on a heavy gaff cutter with a modest rig is the breaking of the boom. I recall sighting along the boom when close reefed and noticing that it was bent out of straight by one diameter, due to the pull of the leech, inboard from the mainsheet. When conditions became more exciting, it was time to break out the trysail, which was of the triangular pattern, and made of heavy flax. It was so heavy, when wet, that we got into the habit of stowing it in the pram dinghy.

One bit of traditional gaff rig seamanship which was found on working boats, but was never 'yacht practice', and is not mentioned by any of today's writers on the gaff rig, is the use of a gaff vang when raising and lowering the mainsail at sea. This practice is seldom seen in old photographs, because it applies when the boat is under way. I have seen one photograph of an Essex smack trawling under sail in the thirties with a gaff vang belayed round the outboard end of the boom, just as HWT did. If the boat carries a topsail, as HWT's boats did not, you can use the topsail sheet as the vang. To sail without one, as most do, is unsafe.

HWT insisted on the use of the gaff vang. In normal weather he saw that the lee topping lift was unhooked and taken forward to the shrouds, along with the lee runner, to reduce chafe, with the gaff vang belayed round the boom, clear of the leech.

I timed the evolutions and it usually took us four minutes to tack *Baroque* and five minutes to gybe her, including hardening in the mainsheet, although HWT usually preferred to go through the wind if it was blowing. I could and did do it singlehanded during night watches in light weather but in general HWT tacked and wore ship at the change of watch. The gaff vang (correctly pronounced 'wang' by HWT) played no role apart from being shortened as the mainsail was roller reefed, until the time came to drop the mainsail at sea, which was done either to reduce chafe in a calm or in order to set the trysail in blowing weather.

The 'drill' was then for the vang to be unhitched from the boom and for the helmsman to trap the vang round a cleat, as taut as possible. The crew members tasked with dropping the mainsail went forward to the mast, set up the topping lift, took the coils of peak and throat halyard off the pins and overhauled them to run freely. At the skipper's command 'Drop' the halyards were let go and paid out over the pins to keep control, with the sheet being hardened in to drop the boom into the permanent gallows as soon as the topping lift was eased, whilst the helmsman hauled in the vang keeping it trapped and taut until the gaff was all the way down and a tyer could be put round it. Until that moment, no-one was to be anywhere between the cockpit and the mast.

This is an essential safety procedure to ensure that nobody is swept overboard by the gaff, which will thrash about as it comes down in a seaway. The death of the great Eric Tabarly, lost from his Fife cutter *Pen Duick* in the Irish Sea, was from ignorance of this precaution by an inexperienced crew.

Baroque had had a wheel, but HWT had abolished this in favour of a very substantial laminated tiller. There were no navigational aids other than the compass, a lead line, a Walker Excelsior IV patent log and HWT's sextant and deck watch. The lack of an echo sounder meant that taking soundings was a cold business in high latitudes, and we used to swap jobs after three casts. HWT, given his Army background, paid me a magnificent back-handed compliment in the book—"Andrew swung the lead like a professional..."

HWT enjoyed navigation, to the point that I recall him pulling out the sextant for a line of position when in sight of land. In ice, he made much use of the ratlines and would, if opportunity offered, anchor under the lee of a rocky island and climb it, to get an even better view. Despite owning a copy of Lecky's *Wrinkles*, I have yet to find HWT's favourite passage, "The navigator knows of no sensation more disagreeable than that of running ashore, unless it be accompanied by a doubt as to which continent the shore belongs to!"

I have no complaints whatever about the food—there was plenty of it and it was good. On those occasions when we had something particular to celebrate—crossing the Arctic Circle, Furthest North, etc., we used to conspire to get HWT to talk—and when we succeeded, by way of a good meal, he was fascinating. I have continued to quote his line "No vessel should be without Tabasco sauce. It adds a relish to the plainest fare, and is probably a powerful germicide."

That sentence—balanced and polished to perfection—leads me to consider HWT the writer. Good writing is achieved by taking pains, and he took them. It is interesting to compare his short accounts in the RCC Journal with the longer ones in these books, to see how he worked up to the finished product. He has been the victim of his own self-deprecating dry humour; people with a less developed sense of fun than his have often missed the jokes.

HWT was very well read—he was of the generation which routinely subscribed to *Blackwood's Magazine*, much read by solitary Englishmen across the Empire, and to which he contributed. I can illustrate this with a story against myself. During a boring anchor watch at Stornoway, I remembered HWT's jokes about verse in the log book on the Heard Island expedition, and wrote out, from memory, in the 'Observations' column of the log, the lines:

Sleepe after toyle, port after stormie seas,
Ease after warre, death after life does greatly please

from Spenser's *The Faerie Queene*. At least, I thought I had, but when I woke again, after turning in, I found that HWT had taken a moment in his watch to silently correct my quotation.

As regards HWT's legendary taciturnity, a passage in a book by Jean Merrien, almost the founding father of modern French yachting, came to my mind. He points out (writing in 1953) that there are no English singlehanders; the English don't need to sail singlehanded "car ils ne parlent pas"! Today, after Chichester, Rose and Knox-Johnson, followed by thousands, we no longer think that there are no British singlehanders, but Merrien's observation holds true; if you are going to be cooped up with a handful of other people for months, the less said, the better. A garrulous person will have bored their companions with repetition by the half-way mark of the journey or the voyage.

The question of HWT's leadership sometimes comes up. He was not a leader in the Eisenhower manner—he was not someone who could organise very complex operations; nor in the Churchill manner—he was not a man who could inspire a nation. He was what I think is termed a leader for objectives. He knew what he wanted to do, he found out how to do it, and he had acquired, through hard work in preparing for it, the ability to cope with whatever Fate threw at him on the way there and back. He led from the front. If you are twenty-something, you are not going to let a man of seventy-something do more than you do. It worked for me; I would have followed him anywhere and I know that goes for many of us who sailed with him.

Looking back across more than forty years, it is rather pleasant to see that HWT is better known now than he was when I crewed for him. He had no interest in publicity, and his voyages got only the occasional paragraph in the yachting press of the day. The print runs of his books were tiny—I believe just two thousand copies of *Triumph and Tribulation*.

The book moves from a major to a minor key—a voyage which was a 'triumph', one that was by HWT's standards a failure, in that the objective was missed, and one that finally convinced HWT to give in to advancing age and put a stop to his voyaging to northern waters in his own boat.

I am able to write this note because I am one of several people who were approached by Simon Richardson to join him aboard *En Avant* and who were unable to raise the cash stake that Simon needed. Nobody can know what happened, but we do know from HWT's letters home from Rio that he had enjoyed the passage and the crew were the best he had sailed with. Let's leave it at that.

He was a man. Take him for all in all.
I shall not look upon his like again.

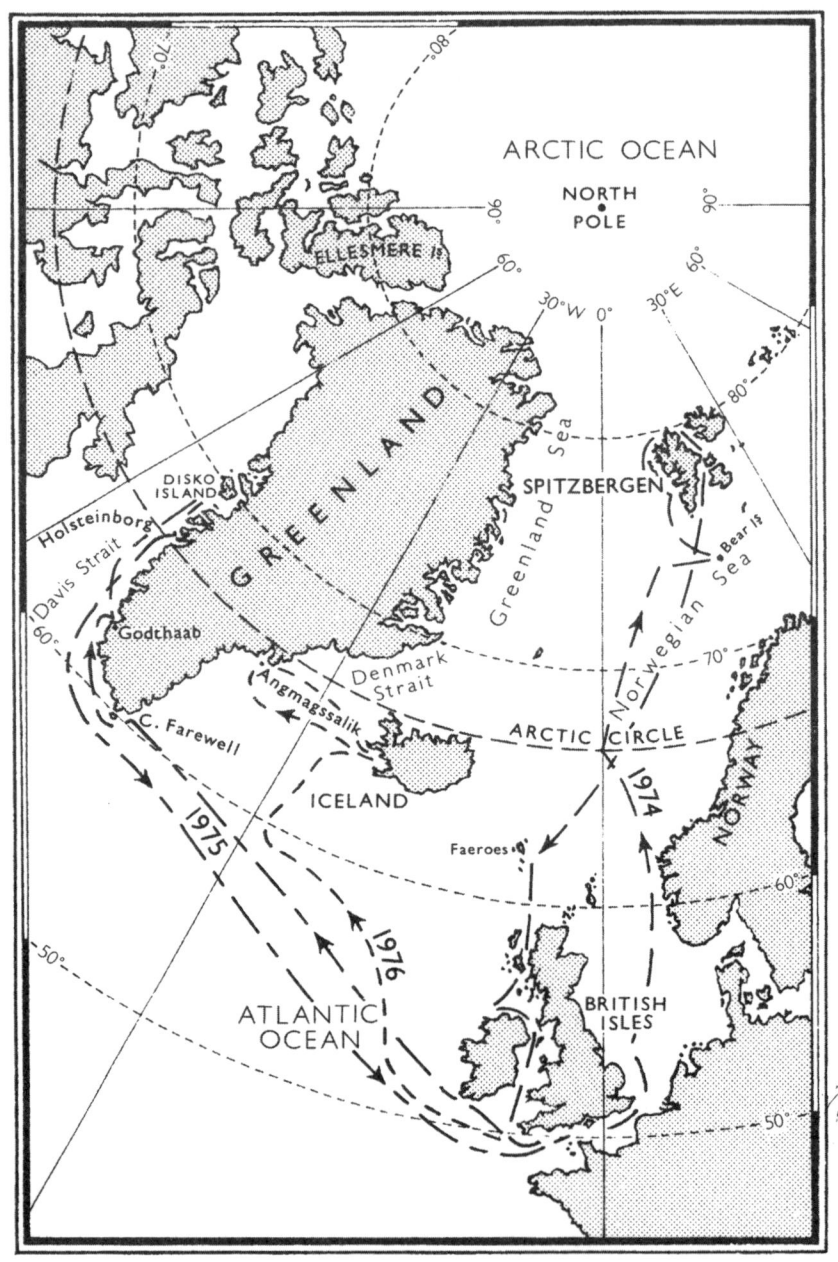

Map 1: Voyages of *Baroque* 1974–1976

PART ONE

Circumnavigation of Spitzbergen

1974

Map 2: Spitzbergen

CHAPTER I

A FRESH START

———————◆———————

COLONEL WILLIAM F. CODY, alias Buffalo Bill, earned his sobriquet by his association with buffaloes, an entirely successful association from the colonel's point of view. Years ago some American climbing friends took it into their heads to label me Himal Bill, a title that no doubt owed more to length of association with the Himalaya than to entire success. Having long since forsaken the Himalaya and instead made ten or more Greenland voyages I might now qualify for the title of Greenland Bill, or perhaps Eskimo Bill, not to be confused with Eskimo Nell, the heroine of a long sexual saga. To make so many voyages to the same region seems to imply a lack of imagination. From my point of view, however, Greenland is the ideal objective, combining remoteness, difficulty of access, the grandest scenery, an inexhaustible number of mountainous fjords each with its own character, and on the whole a region still sufficiently unfrequented for a man in a small boat to feel very remotely akin to the early sea-men-explorers and to their successors the old whaling men from Hull, Leith, Dundee; and should he chance to find himself in difficulties among ice, to share in a much milder way their harsh experiences. All this being so, why go elsewhere? As the man from Texas advised: 'When you strike ile stop boring.'

Greenland had for me become a habit and habits are difficult to break. In 1974, however, we at last got out of the rut by going to Spitzbergen. Some might think this a change for the worse since it involved sailing much further north, so far north in fact that at one point we were within 600 miles of the North Pole. Though this proximity is illusory, since the 600 miles comprise mainly rough ice broken by leads of open water, it accounts for Spitzbergen having been chosen in the past as the jumping-off place for several attempts to reach the Pole, attempts that were remarkable for the variety of means employed. In 1827, from a base on the north coast, Parry and his naval party made their effort by man-hauling the specially fitted ship's boats. In 1897 Andrée began his fatal balloon flight from Danes Island at the north-west corner of Spitzbergen. Amundsen, in 1925, used two Dornier flying-boats; and in 1928, starting from Ny Alesund on the west coast, Nobile crashed the airship *Italia* on the return flight and in the subsequent search for the missing airship Amundsen lost his life. Finally, in 1931, Sir Hubert Wilkins, ahead of his time, used a submarine. In two of these ventures several lives were lost, and all except Parry's seemed designed to prove the capabilities of a particular form of transport.

Besides its proximity to the Pole Spitzbergen enjoys another feature that recommended it as a base for these sorties. In spite of the high latitude (up to 80° N.) the whole of the west coast is free from ice throughout the summer, and from July onwards the greater part of the north coast as well. Nowhere else in the world can a small, unstrengthened vessel safely reach so high a latitude, so that for anyone with the urge to penetrate remote regions, preferably mountainous, Spitzbergen is a powerful magnet and an obvious objective. For ten years it had figured high on my list but for one reason or another a visit had been deferred. For one thing, except on the east coast where access is less simple, it is all well known and, as Belloc says, when the unknown becomes known 'it loses that mysterious power of attraction which the unknown always possesses'. From early in the 17th century all the fjords, bays, and coves along the west coast were known and used by the whalers, mostly Dutch and British. When the whales and the whalers disappeared early in the 18th century Russian and Norwegian trappers appeared on the scene, nor did they confine themselves, like the whalers, to the coastal regions. In the present century expeditions to Spitzbergen have been numerous, particularly in the 'twenties and 'thirties when parties from Oxford and Cambridge worked there, crossing and recrossing it and no doubt climbing most of the mountains. And if all this were not enough there are the visiting cruise ships, starting with the *Lusitania* as far back as 1894—a predecessor of the famous Cunarder of that name, built in 1903 and sunk by a German submarine in 1915.

Unlike Greenland, Spitzbergen has never had any indigenous population. Excluding those employed in the five or six coal-mines,

which are worked all the year round, it is uninhabited. Yet Greenland, for most Europeans, is less well known, owing presumably to
the absence there of any cruise ships; at least there have been none
until this year (1974) when, I believe, a trial run was made to the
west coast. The presence of ice on both the Greenland coasts is a
discouraging factor for this kind of activity. On the other hand far
fewer climbing parties go to Spitzbergen than to Greenland which,
so much vaster, is enormously rich in mountains; nor do the comparatively few Spitzbergen peaks rank with those of Greenland for
either stature, beauty, or climbing interest. The highest are in the
interior where they are more like nunataks projecting from a miniature ice-cap—Mt. Newton 5445 ft. is the highest—while those border-
ing the fjords within striking distance of a boat party, while steep
and Alpine in character, are from only 2000 ft. to 3000 ft. high. Here,
perhaps, was another reason for deferring my visit. No mountains
are to be despised—what a world it would be were there none—yet
ten years ago I may have felt that mountains of such modest height
were below my standard, whereas by 1974, my altitude ceiling falling fast, they were just about my mark or even a little above it.
Merit may be acquired merely by reaching some remote region,
yet a voyage with an objective beyond that of getting there and
back safely has more flavour, and for a mountaineer the objective
is obviously mountains. In recent voyages therefore, since my own
ardour and ability have diminished, I have always tried to include
in the crew two climbers to undertake the serious climbing, leaving
me free to potter on easier ground. Since nearly all the fjords on
the west coast of Spitzbergen are littered with mountains we had a
wide choice and would happily take whatever offered. In fact on this
voyage climbing was a secondary objective. What I really wanted to
do was to circumnavigate the island, a task harder to achieve probably than any of the mountains.

Unless we have been to a place our ideas of its geography are
probably a little scattered. Spitzbergen, for instance, we all know of
though strictly speaking there is no such place. The island I wanted
to sail round is called Vestspitzbergen while the whole group or archipelago is known as Svalbard. The following quotation from the Arctic
Pilot explains matters:

This ancient name (Svalbard) was first given nearly nine hundred years ago to a land discovered by the 'Northmen' some four days sail northward of Iceland, and from time to time there has been considerable controversy as to its exact location.

It is claimed that in all probability the archipelago was discovered by the Norwegians in 1194, and re-discovered by the Dutch navigator Barents in 1596. The English explorer Henry Hudson visited Svalbard in 1607.

In the Middle Ages all polar lands were held to be part of, or at least belong to, Greenland, and the separateness of the two was not really determined until 1707, while the real circumnavigation of Vestspitzbergen was first performed by the Norwegian Elling Carlsen in 1863. The present Svalbard originates with the Treaty of Paris, 1920, by which measure the sovereignty of all lands embraced within the area between the parallels of Lat. 74 N. and 81 N. and the meridians of Long. 10 E. and 35 E. was vested in Norway. In August 1925 the Norwegian Government formally inaugurated their administration by sending an official, who hoisted their flag over the group, renaming it Svalbard.

Svalbard thus includes Vestspitzbergen, Nordaustlandet, Barentsoya, Edgeoya, Prins Karls Forland, and the islets lying close to them, together with the smaller islands of Bjornoya, Hopen, Kong Karlsland, and Kvitoya.

Besides Elling Carlsen mentioned above as having circumnavigated Vestspitzbergen, another circumnavigator under sail was Frank Stuart Worsley, a professional seaman, who had been Shackleton's navigator on the famous voyage in the ship's lifeboat *James Caird* from Elephant Is. in the South Shetlands to South Georgia. But Worsley's track lay along the north coast of Vestspitzbergen, thence south to a point about half-way through Hinlopen Strait, and then counter-clockwise round Nordaustlandet, a far more difficult feat as there is usually a lot of ice east and north of Nordaustlandet. Worsley's vessel was the 100-ton trading barque *Island*, sheathed with steel plates forward for ice protection. He had with him an amateur crew of twelve. In the process they lost the propeller and so damaged the rudder that having got back to their starting point in Isfjord they finally accepted a tow to Norway.

It is time to introduce *Baroque*, the Bristol Channel pilot cutter that I had acquired in 1973 in place of *Sea Breeze*. The same year we sailed her to West Greenland. Before that voyage she had needed some attention, and after it she needed a lot more. She had been built in 1902 when the pilots based on Bristol Channel ports owned and sailed their own boats. After the First War, with the advent of steam, the pilot-age service was put on a different footing, and the cutters, some sixty of them, were sold, many of them for conversion into yachts. It is now lost, but I once had a list of them and the prices they fetched—*Mischief*, for example, which I owned from 1954 until 1968, went for £350 and the top price was about £500. This sounds little enough but for today's money the figures would have to be multiplied by at least ten. One would like to know something about the pilot who gave his boat the curious name of *Baroque*, and why. According to the dictionary the word means whimsical, grotesque, irregular in shape. Grotesque might describe the doghouse which some misguided owner has stuck on her, but that is an addition of recent date. Pilot cutters had either a flush deck or perhaps a low cabin skylight. As for irregularity, detractors with keen eyes, viewing her sideways on, might point to her irregular sheer-line which sags a little amidships as if she were feeling tired. Which is not to be wondered at, though personally, I think the wavy sheerline gives her a rakish look. Nevertheless she is of a different shape to that of my two earlier boats, *Mischief* and *Sea Breeze*. She has less beam for a greater length, the bows are finer and more cutaway, and she is harder in the bilge. These finer lines do not seem to make her sail any faster than her predecessors while they markedly reduce the space on deck, particularly the foredeck, as well as the amount of stowage space below. However, in 1973 I had to take what I could get and with boats, as with women and horses, one must be 'to their faults a little blind, and to their virtues ever kind'. Always speak well of the bridge that has carried one over. There are not many boats built in 1902 that are still going strong or even going at all, and none that has sailed, as *Baroque* has, to Lat. 80° N.

On her first Greenland voyage she had proved a little wet; in fact a leak amidships under the galley floor might have been described by an oil-man as a gusher. On her return the leaks had to be stopped and some of the frames in way of the mast needed replacing or doubling.

The chainplates on the starboard side had to be lengthened and a new keelband fitted. A jagged break in the keelband had contributed to our having become firmly enmeshed in a salmon net in Davis Strait. All this took time and March had arrived before the hull was being stopped preparatory to a coat of anti-fouling and her return into the water. Either from curiosity or too much zeal one of the men so employed stuck his knife clean through the hull between two planks. Mindful of their unhappy experience with *Sea Breeze* under similar circumstances the Yard hastened to give me the news by telephone and suggested a survey. In the winter of 1968–9 *Sea Breeze*, the Pilot Cutter I had just acquired in place of *Mischief*, had been hauled out for several months for a major overhaul during which no one had thought of examining the caulking. Sailing in May as usual for Greenland, while we were held up in the Solent for two days by strong westerlies, the caulking fell out piecemeal, and she had finally to be slipped again and recaulked throughout. So this time I asked my friend John Tew,* a surveyor, to have a look at the boat and I arranged to meet him in the yard. He had been concerned—in both senses of the word—over *Mischief* and *Sea Breeze* and naturally did not expect to find *Baroque* any more free from the ravages of time than they had been. When we met on the slipway where the boat was hauled out John Tew had finished his inspection. I could divine, without waiting to be told, that his news was bad:

> Yea, this man's brow, like to a title-leaf,
> Foretells the nature of a tragic volume.

The recaulking of the hull, a breast-hook to hold the bows together, and extra fastenings to make sure the coach-roof remained in place, were his minimum requirements. There were others but with the time and money available only these could be accepted, and even with these done John Tew, an exacting man, could not think of any class at Lloyds for which *Baroque* would qualify. The fact that we were bound for Arctic waters had to be considered. No waters are fool-proof and northern waters are less so than most. In the matter of weather, however, I should doubt if up there in summer the weather is any more inclement than around the British Isles.

---

* John Tew died in October 1975.

This additional, unexpected expense was profoundly discouraging. It gave me a shock and like the shock treatment that leaves alcoholics with a disgust for alcohol, it almost extinguished my liking for old wooden boats or even for the sea. Why not retire to the middle of some continent, preferably mountainous, where the call of the sea would be inaudible. But hope springs eternal in even my breast and the gloom cast by this costly business was lightened by a satisfactory settlement of the crew problem, that annually recurring headache which often is not settled until the last moment and then not without misgivings.

Given a good crew the boat's shortcomings are of less moment while with a poor crew the ablest of boats seldom goes far. Simon Richardson, who had been a tower of strength on the previous voyage, wanted to come again, and in two volunteers from Yorkshire, Paul Reinsch and Alan Stockdale, who had sailed and climbed together, I felt I had two capable and reliable hands. We met on board one week-end during the winter and while this did not allow me to assess their respective characters and their likely behaviour at sea, at least it allowed them to assess the boat. Although a psychologist may think he can, in my experience a witch or a wizard is no more likely to divine a man's character and his suitability for a given task from a brief meeting. Such a meeting merely assures one that the man is blessed with the usual number of eyes and limbs, how he may react after a month or two's subjection to the strains and stresses imposed by the confined life in a small boat is but guesswork; unless, of course, having had ocean-going experience, he knows what to expect and what will be expected of him. Paul was a craftsman and knowledgeable about engines. He himself maintained a small boat at Whitehaven in which he and Alan had made a most enterprising voyage to St. Kilda and thence to the small island of Rhona north of Cape Wrath. Both were keen climbers, well versed in modern technique and ironmongery, accustomed to camping and roughing it.

For the first time for many years I had not even had to advertise for a cook, a post that is not easy to fill and not often filled to the satisfaction of everyone. Apart from standing no watches and having all night in, the cook, if he is up to his job, will find he has more work to do than anyone. A Cambridge undergraduate in his last year, Andrew Craig-Bennett, wrote to ask if I had a vacant berth. With the three I already had the only vacancy left was that of cook and when I had explained this to Andrew he gladly agreed to come in that capacity. He sounded to me the right sort so we omitted the formality of meeting, a formality, as I have said, of questionable value. He kept a boat of his own on the East coast where intricate shoals, short seas, and a harsh climate combine to form a rigorous training ground for amateur sailors. My only regret was that his experience would be more useful on deck than in the galley.

Thus a month before sailing day the boat was back in the water and I had what looked like a capable and experienced crew, so much so that I could promise myself an easy time, lying below reading mind-broadening literature, dodging the drips, digesting the duffs that Andrew would no doubt provide, and appearing on deck at infrequent intervals to take a sight. Such a complacent feeling of well-being—hubris, I think, is the word—is often the prelude to a change of fortune. Simon wrote to say that owing to the sudden death of his father he would have to withdraw. Thus, having no reserves in hand or even in sight, I went down to Lymington in mid-May in a thoughtful or even subdued mood. None of the feelers hastily put out had so far touched anything and it was late in the day to start advertising. Something might be hoped for from time and chance, factors upon which I have come to rely heavily, but time was short.

The two clear days I had before the crew started to arrive were spent replacing the wooden ratlines with rope. Although at Mylor the previous year the projecting ends had been sawn off they still stuck out far enough beyond the shrouds for the halyards to catch on them in a maddening way. I regretted having to do this because wooden ratlines always look neat whereas rope stretches and sags, and if much time has to be spent aloft, when navigating among ice, for example, wood is easier on the feet. The crew arrived on 20th May and we soon had the spars shipped and the rigging rove, leaving ample time for the innumerable, unforeseen jobs that keep cropping up when a boat is being got ready for sea.

Paul and Alan drove from Yorkshire in a car that Paul in a fit of extravagance unusual in Yorkshiremen had bought for £15. If he could keep that going, I reflected, he should have no difficulty with our engine. During the winter my friend Colin Putt, an engineering maestro from Australia, had put in a lot of work, among other things installing two new fuel tanks. The old ones were merely two forty-gallon oil drums which had rusted abominably. Colin replaced these with two of heavier gauge treated inside and out against rust. While fitting out we had a visitor, a tolerably ancient mariner, who told us that he had once owned *Baroque*, having come by her cheaply, in fact for nothing. Unwanted, neglected, she had been allowed to sink at her moorings in Cowes harbour. After some time under water she had been raised by our friend who for his trouble had been told to keep her. One could not help wondering whether the engine now installed had undergone this water cure.

Work progressed and sailing day approached without our coming any nearer to finding a fourth hand. The other three, who had not tried it, talked nonchalantly of sailing short-handed. The few likely coverts that I knew had been drawn blank and to advertise at this late stage, even if successful, involved inevitable delay. The uninstructed might think that at a place like Lymington which more or less revolves round yachts—a thousand or so berthed there would be a conservative estimate—there would be a queue of eager applicants for a free holiday of four months at sea. I knew better. 'I have no great hopes of Birmingham,' Mrs. Elton remarked, 'there's something dire about the sound of it.' Similarly I had no great hopes of Lymington. There may be nothing dire about the sound of it but I suspected that its yachting fraternity, wedded to modern boats, might think there was something dire about the sound of *Baroque*.

On this occasion those fickle allies time and chance did not fail us. About four days before we were due to sail a young Irishman, David White, turned up, having heard of our pressing need either through Simon Richardson or a friend of Simon's whom he had met in a bar. Bar acquaintances are not necessarily suspect, much depends on the bar. In *Mischief*'s time, when two surveyors had condemned her, I had greatly benefited from the advice of one such chance-met acquaintance. David looked about eighteen but was in fact twenty-five and had some unspecified job in Harrods. He knew nothing of the sea or of boats, had no special skills, and indeed nothing to recommend him except a cheerful smile, our sore need, and the fact that he could quit his job and be ready in time. With the three responsible men I already had I could well afford to include one greenhorn and on past occasions have had to be content with a far less favourable ratio. So I took him on and needless to say, later that same day I had an offer from a much more promising candidate whom I had to refuse. It had been touch and go, nor was I confident that David would join as promised. He seemed a volatile character, as bar acquaintances are apt to be.

CHAPTER II

TO BEAR ISLAND

D AVID KEPT HIS WORD and we sailed on 1st June according to plan. As the great Von Moltke observed, few plans withstand contact with the enemy. If they do, and the enemy in this case was time, it is all the more satisfying. Casting off at the start of a long voyage is a pregnant moment, for me pregnant with doubts; doubts even about the wisdom of the voyage, of the crew, of the skipper himself, or whether some vital item has not been forgotten. Above all I was worried by horrid remembrances of *Baroque*'s behaviour on several occasions on her first voyage under power; particularly when we had attempted to leave Umanak, a small harbour with a narrow entrance, the entrance encumbered with grounded bergs, and a stiff breeze blowing directly in. After just missing hitting first a berg and then a rock we returned to our moorings and finally had to be towed out. The large propeller seemed to be so far offset on the port side that even with full contrary helm she edged constantly to starboard. To turn to port the engine had to be in neutral and with any sort of head wind, as at Umanak, she became unmanageable. To counteract this awkward tendency Colin Putt had made a drogue, a small sea-anchor with a heavy iron frame, to be streamed from midships on the port side to about level with the propeller. In theory the drag of this would turn her head to port. There had been no opportunity for a rehearsal and Lymington river, thick with yachts and the occasional ferry, seemed no place for an unrehearsed performance. Instead we took a tow through the narrowest part between the ferry stage and the Marina where the fairway is about twenty yards wide, and then, with prayers to the river gods and encouraging noises to *Baroque*, we cast off the tow-line. Men and women sometimes behave in unexpected ways, so do boats. Feeling, perhaps, that the eyes of England, or at least Lymington, were upon her *Baroque* played no tricks and answered the helm well enough. I had no difficulty in sticking to the strait and narrow path. At the river mouth we hoisted sail and turned east, bound for the North Sea, first stop Bear Island.

Frank Bullen, in *The Cruise of the Cachalot*, records that the old sperm-whaling ships, mostly American (one of them, by the way, is preserved in the Marine Museum at Mystic, Connecticut), in the course of voyages that might last two or three years, seldom called at any port. They avoided ports like the plague. All that they needed to replenish was water and the captain took care to do this at some remote, uninhabited island—Aldabra, for example, where the crew had neither the temptation nor the opportunity to desert. It is an example that I have found it advisable to follow in so far as to avoid if possible, a call at any port on the way out. Bound for East Greenland, for instance, it would be wiser not to call at Iceland. Bear Is. is only some 200 miles short of Spitzbergen, and while its name and its remoteness alike demanded a visit on our part, I reckoned it far enough from home to be, as it were, a point of no return should any of the crew by then be having second thoughts.

We made a brisk start, passing Dungeness at noon next day. The same evening, with Calais in sight, we went about to begin the long haul to the north, from Lat. 50° N. to Lat. 75° N., some fifteen hundred miles as the crow flies and no doubt many more as *Baroque* would sail. Even at that early stage it seemed likely that David would never be of much use on deck, whereas Andrew, who between spells in the galley lent us an able hand, would obviously be in his element. I therefore arranged for them to change places, a step that required some self-denial. The few days of Andrew's reign in the galley had been so brilliant that it seemed the act of a madman or of a sour ascetic to cut it short, while if David were to show as little aptitude in the galley as he had on deck we faced lean times. At the moment Paul and Alan were indifferent to food having not yet found their sea-legs. They would not notice any difference between the master's dishes and those that would now be served up by the apprentice. But besides cooking food Andrew had an amazing ability to eat it, while I, too, liked my victuals and am not over fond of resisting temptation where food is concerned. At sea, at any rate, where priorities are easily determined, one can agree with Epicurus that the beginning and root of all good is the pleasure of the stomach; even wisdom and culture must be referred to this.

Those twin topics food and seasickness must, I'm afraid, loom large in the early stages of any voyage. Paul was our chief sufferer. For many days even a moderately rough sea laid him out, so many that I became concerned, fearful that he might prove to be another chronic case for whom use and wont is no cure. For more than a fortnight he ate little enough and looked accordingly wan and spectre-like. However once the corner had been turned he reacted strongly, almost startlingly, making up for past omissions and speedily overhauling or out-eating Andrew who until then had been our chief cormorant. The contest between these two was stubborn. Andrew did not surrender the crown easily but the writing was on the wall when Paul assumed what hitherto had been Andrew's prerogative, taking care of anything left over and scraping the bottoms of the pans. Neither of them went as far as Sherpas do, holding the plate up to the face and licking it, or if mugs were being used, as for pemmican soup or tea and tsumpa, then polishing out the mug with the forefinger and licking that. We had with us some copies of *The Times* which had accumulated at Lymington where I had not had the leisure for battling with the crossword puzzles. Doing them now, seeking inspiration from the adjacent Personal Column, my eye lit on a curious notice. I showed it to Paul and Andrew and stuck it in the log-book in case they wanted to follow it up when they got back: 'Anorexia Nervosa, Compulsive fasting, stuffing. Box No...'

On the 3rd, the wind fresh and free, we passed the Galloper light vessel. When the wind died we ran the engine in order to learn what effect Colin Putt's patent steering drogue would have. She certainly required a little less help to keep her straight but as we had found when coming down Lymington river the fault had largely corrected itself. Her improved steering when under power as compared with the previous voyage is another unsolved sea mystery. Becalmed once more on the following day, not far from the Dogger Bank, we caught two nice cod on the bottom in twenty fathoms, and later two mackerel also from deep down. Fish and chips for supper followed by a duff of Andrew's making, for David was still feeling his way, and frequently stumbling, among the foothills of cookery, far from the gastronomic heights.

If the navigator is asked by one of the crew where the ship is, he feels obliged to commit himself or at least hazard a guess. On the other hand, if he is not asked and he thinks he knows where he is, he should not let pride tempt him into announcing to a suitably awe-struck crew what sea-mark or cape they will presently sight and where, or, as in this instance, what they will not sight. But every ass loves to hear himself bray. I thought we were too far east to sight Smith's Knoll light vessel and rashly imparted this unimportant piece of knowledge to the crew. No one unkindly reminded me of this. It was humiliation enough to read later the log-book entry to the effect that we had left that particular light vessel close to port at 4 a.m. Soon after breakfast we sighted a Shell-Esso gas platform and were in fact carried rather too close to it by a strong tide. A helicopter landed on it as we passed. For the Dogger area where we now were a gale warning had been put out. About force six was all the wind we had and enough, too, for Paul and Alan to succumb and for David to experience some mishaps in the galley. Scalded cats are a common and reliable standard for judging leaping powers, and since David's back where the kettle landed had not been scalded, nor even marked, the leap he gave, and the accompanying yell, were the more remarkable. After this, and in the prevailing conditions, he did well to produce sausage and mash for supper, even if the sausages had to be scraped off the floor. Like onions, no ship should be without Tabasco Sauce. It gives a relish to the plainest fare and is probably a powerful germicide.

On the whole by the end of our first week at sea, in spite of Paul's persistent sickness and frequent bad news from the galley, I felt reasonably satisfied. We were well up the North Sea, about 150 miles east of Dundee and a like distance from the southern coast of Norway. The boat was drier as, of course, she should have been after recaulking and with a newly painted deck; but in any seaway she made quite a bit of water and there were still enough drips from the deckhead to be annoying. Plastic sheeting and drawing pins were again in demand. One reason for contentment lay in the crew who were cheerful, hardworking, and apparently enjoying themselves. In this last respect I was mistaken. A week had been enough for young David who now asked to be put ashore, life at sea falling short of his expectations and the prospect of months more of it quite insupportable. Request not granted. Quite apart from the replacement problem, probably insoluble, we could not afford to waste days beating to some port in Scotland, still less did I want to visit the complicated Norwegian coast of which I had charts only for the most northerly part. In a small crew the presence of one unhappy, unwilling member may well cause trouble. Happily I had no need to worry about that. The other three had the success of the voyage at heart as much as I had, that and the safety of the ship were all that mattered to them.

In Lat. 57° N., Long. 03° E., about ninety miles off the Norwegian coast, we sighted an enormous concrete island, a miniature town crowned by a chimney that almost rivalled that of Fawley, belching a flame of natural gas. Whatever one may think of the consequences of North Sea oil, some good, some possibly dire, or of the curious conviction of the Scots or their loud-mouthed spokesmen, that they not only put the stuff there in the first place, but rediscovered it, provided the money and the know-how to sink the wells and bring it ashore, the sight of these man-made islands are astonishing testimonies to the enterprise and technical skill of twentieth-century man, led, to be honest, by Americans. The North Sea is no tranquil lake and the skill and seamanship needed to site precisely and then build these structures is almost beyond belief.

A man describing a passage such as this through well-known waters, unless he can paint in words the ever-changing scene of sea and sky in faint imitation of a Conrad, is reduced to recording trivial events such as the making up of a Norwegian courtesy flag which we had forgotten to bring. Sufficient red, white, and blue bunting were obtained by cutting up signal flags (which we were never likely to use) and we had made careful note of the right way to combine these colours from the occasional Norwegian vessel that passed with its ensign flying. After doing the rough groundwork I handed it over to Paul who was a much better hand with a needle. Then there was the curious encounter with the German tanker from Hamburg which having passed ahead of us westbound, when two miles away turned round and steamed straight back towards us. As he passed for the second time I hailed him with the loudspeaker—'Are you all right?'—a question usually asked by the steamer of the yacht. We got no answer.

We read in Shakespeare of 'the poet's eye, in a fine frenzy rolling', similarly though more coarsely, when writing of these voyages I am occasionally able to make my own mouth water (and perhaps the

mouths of a few equally uncouth readers) by recollecting some of the
more memorable meals we enjoyed. In fact had I but a less defective
memory and more descriptive powers it would be a grateful task in
the long winter evenings of old age to compile a book of memorable
meals—*Gleanings of a Glutton*, or some such title. A similar thing, more
wholesome and less enervating, might be done for one's memorable
bathes. But on this outward voyage, I'm afraid, meals were memorable only for the wrong reason—things improved immensely on the
way home—and had it not been for Andrew hovering and helping in
the background we had fared but ill. At sea the punctuality of meal-
times is important, so that the man going on watch can have his meal
beforehand, and the man coming off can have his before it gets cold.
This calls for careful timing on the part of the cook and as yet David's
timing was erratic. His first attempt to down us with a duff, a praise-
worthy ambition, led to the stew appearing an hour-and-a-half late
at 9 p.m. Having coated himself and the galley floor with flour and
squeezed the remnants into the largest available saucepan, he found
he had no room on the stove for that and the stew. We could, of course,
have had the pudding first like they do in Iceland, there is no need to
be hide-bound in these matters. On another occasion a delay of two
hours was explained by the belated discovery that he had filled the
stove with methylated spirit instead of paraffin, a sort of Irish bull.
Flour, I admit, is intractable stuff and in the hands of the amateur
liable to spread itself. In the Himalaya after the day's march, I used
to turn to and make bread, inside a tent if it happened to be raining.
Emerging from the tent on one occasion, my boots white with flour,
the inference was obvious, and henceforward my loaves were known
as 'Foot-bread'. But as I have said, when David's vagaries became too
much for Andrew, threatening to thwart his over-keen appetite, he
took charge of the supper to our great benefit as well as his. Bully beef
pie followed by syrup tart and baked custard is a random example that
obviously bears his signature. He also tried to impress upon David the
necessity of keeping things in their proper place, the galley shelves
rapidly becoming a hurrah's nest, everything on top and nothing to
hand; and having taken a degree in English he painted on the galley
shelf in large letters, misquoting Shakespeare, 'Every item has a local
habitation and a name.'

By the end of the second week we had not done so well. Head winds and short, steep seas, followed by a bout of hot, windless, anticyclonic weather slowed us down and pushed us close to the Norwegian coast. We logged only 280 miles in the week and by no means all of that was in the right direction. By then we had finished the fresh bread and had started on what I call the 'hard-bake'—bread that after slicing is re-baked. This lot had been cut too thick, baked too long, and was abominably hard. Instead of a bread-knife we used a fret-saw. By the 13th we had drifted to within ten miles of the coast south of Bergen, the barometer as high as ever at 1030 mbs., no wind and no signs of any. We enjoyed sun and sea bathing but at the end of the third windless day it occurred to me to check our water supply. The main tank proved to be nearly dry, implying that we had used some four gallons a day instead of the normal allowance of two and a half gallons. More probably the header tank which supplies the main tank, owing to an air-lock, had not been full when we started. The tank that lurks beneath the cabin table, thus keeping cool those who sit round the table, was untouched so that we had twenty days supply in hand. Bear Is. was still some 700 miles away. Assuming the worst, that our daily average did not improve, it would be a close-run thing; but we were getting a good lift from the Norwegian current which sets north up the coast, and the spell of calm weather, unequalled in these latitudes in my experience, must soon end. The 'hard-bake', too, needed to be conserved. We cut out bread for breakfast and David tried his hand successfully at soda-bread, his native product. Is it possible that the daily intake of bicarbonate of soda in his bread accounts for an Irishman's effervescent behaviour?

In N. Lat. 65° the fine weather packed up and we were to enjoy no more until close to Spitzbergen. Bear Is. and the seas for a long way south are noted for overcast skies and fog. After carrying a fresh southwesterly wind all night, by midday of the 21st we had logged eighty-four miles and I reckoned that by tea-time we should be north of the Arctic Circle. Accordingly we began our celebrations in time by having a slug of whisky in our tea. Shortly after a hail from on deck gave us the welcome news that Father Neptune, or his Arctic representative, had come on board, apparently over the bows. By coincidence I had just made some baggy wrinkle for the topping lifts to save the mainsail from chafe and except for this round the waist he was naked, but the flippers on his feet, goggles, crown and trident, and a red beard, together made up a striking ensemble. He concluded a short, seamanlike speech of welcome by presenting me with a scroll, the necessary passport giving us the freedom of his domain. In return I gave him what the French call 'un grand coup de whisky', for in spite of being native to those parts he was obviously feeling cold. Andrew took charge of the subsequent banquet which comprised *risotto Bolognese*, alleviated by prunes and baked custard.

Even in the vicinity of N. Lat. 70° it was less cold than might be expected, less cold than it would have been in that latitude off Greenland, owing no doubt to the Norwegian current still running from the south. The sea temperature did not drop appreciably until we met what is called the Spitzbergen current which runs west out of the cold Barents Sea. As usual on these voyages we were keeping a weather log for the Meteorological Office. Obviously we cannot transmit our observations at the time as does the great fleet of Voluntary Observing Ships—some 500 Selected ships and fifty Supplementary ships—but in the absence of any observations at all from waters little frequented by British ships our observations are of use for the records and are always welcome at Bracknell. Every six hours we recorded wind, cloud, visibility, pressure, air and sea temperatures. At the Arctic Circle the sea temperature was 55° F and had fallen to 39° F by the time we reached Bear Is. In a war-time debate about maritime affairs in which the subject of shark repellent had been mentioned, Winston Churchill took the opportunity to remark that 'His Majesty's Government was totally opposed to sharks'. As might be expected from a modern edition of Col. Blimp I am totally opposed to the metric system and since the thermometers provided by Bracknell are graduated in Centigrade I have taken the trouble to translate back into Fahrenheit. Most of us had already donned our winter woollies and when the wind permitted we had the cabin heater lit. With much wind or the mainsail sheeted in, the down draught off the sail proved too much for the cabin heater and we had to do without. Besides colder water, the Spitzbergen current brings with it a lot of driftwood, massive logs brought down by rivers from the forests of Siberia. The east coast of Jan Mayen Is. is thickly strewn with such logs

and hardly any of the Svalbard beaches that we visited were without
their quota. On dark nights in a rough sea these great logs might be
a hazard to a small vessel of light construction, but in these high latitudes it is late in the autumn before the nights get dark when no such
vessels are likely to be about.

Before reaching Bear Is. we had some roughish weather. On three
occasions in the last week of June we were either hove-to or lying-a-try,
that is to say lying broadside on with no sails set. All this wind came
from an easterly quarter so that by the 29th we had been set down
nearly a hundred miles west of the island, so far that I was tempted
to give it up and carry on for Spitzbergen in spite of water problems.
Happily the easterlies subsided, the sea fell calm, and as we began
making up lost ground the problem of finding Bear Is. began to loom
large. Nowadays the navigator has to know only his own position, his
objective's position being definitely fixed; but before the days of chro-
nometers and Admiralty charts the navigator must have had as much
or more doubt about the position of the island or cape he hoped to
make as he had about the position of his ship, a consideration that
makes the voyages of those days even more a cause for astonishment
and admiration. Owing to the prevailing overcast our last noon sight
for latitude had been two days before, and on the evening of the 30th
a single snap sight from a fleeting glimpse of sun had put us twenty
miles west of our dead reckoning position. With no certainty about our
latitude this sight might well be far out.

Early on the morning of 1st July we handed the sails, there being
no wind to speak of, and after breakfast started the engine and kept it
going ruthlessly in the spirit of 'Pike's Peak or bust'. Assuming that
our latitude was correct I determined to get into what I hoped would
be the same longitude as Bear Is. and then steer north, trusting largely
to Providence and to a lesser extent to birds. As the *Pilot* observes:

> At this time of year (summer) the island swarms with guillemots, and
> the flocks of these birds and the direction of their flight are of great
> use to vessels attempting to make Bjornoya in thick weather.

Which was exactly our position, for throughout the day we were pestered by drifting banks of fog. I spent hours on deck on the slight

chance of the sun appearing and the still slighter chance that when it did the horizon immediately below would be clear. It did appear once for about ten seconds, long enough to take a sight, had not the horizon been indistinguishable, leaden-hued sky merging into leaden-hued sea, with no telling where one began or the other ended.

The guillemots had certainly increased in numbers—we felt we were getting warm—but were flying in all directions searching for food rather than Bear Is. Indeed in the prevailing calm conditions and no hours of darkness why should they bother to go home to roost. We would watch a flock set out purposefully as if it had to get there before closing time only to see it alight about half a mile away, merely changing its feeding ground. In one of Neville Shute's best stories, *Trustee from the Tool-room*, there is a character who successfully navigates his small boat from San Francisco to Hawaii by watching aeroplanes and birds. The vapour trails of planes are, I should think, better guides than birds; one could certainly sail from New York, say, and arrive at Shannon by following them.

In order to have supper in peace we stopped the engine. We had finished our sausage and mash and were contemplating a noble duff, David by now having mastered the art, when from on deck came the cry of 'Land'. Sure enough, its top just showing over a bank of fog, there could be seen the hard, black outline of a high rock. It was Stappen, the 610 ft. high stack lying off the south end of Bear Island, some five miles away and broad on the port bow. Whether attributable to luck rather than skill, a landfall such as this gives the small boat sailor unbounded pleasure. The doubt, the long suspense, and then the satisfaction and thrill of seeing this slender black pinnacle floating above the fog, the island itself still completely hidden. For me it compensated for some hideous mistakes of the past and even took some of the sting out of the Smith's Knoll episode. Among some memorable landfalls it reminded me of our first sighting of Heard Is. in the Southern Ocean when from forty miles away the snow-capped summit of Big Ben (9005 ft.) appeared framed in a patch of blue in the middle of a great cumulus cloud high above the sea.

Against a strong west-going current we made slow progress towards Stappen so we altered course to north in order to round the north-west corner of the island. The Norwegian weather station

Nordhamm, for which we were making, lies about half-way along the north coast. Closer in to the shore there were several trawlers about, for the island lies at the southern end of the Spitzbergen Bank which is a rich fishing ground. The *Arctic Pilot* has this description:

> Bjornoya, the southernmost island of Svalbard, lies about 140 miles SSE of the southern point of Vestspitzbergen and about 225 miles NNW of the northern coast of Norway. It is triangular in shape with the apex pointing southwards and it is about 9 miles long and 8 miles wide. The northern part is a plateau 110 ft. to 150 ft. high cut up by numerous shallow lakes, the coast being bounded by vertical cliffs. The south-eastern and southern parts are mountainous, the east coast being dominated by Miseryfjellet, a table mountain 1758 ft. high. The southern part of the island is also bounded by almost vertical cliffs, which in places reach an elevation of 1300 ft. In many places there are beaches at the foot of the cliffs on which landing can be affected but only in exceptionally favourable weather. Owing, however, to the very steep cliffs, it is only in a few places that access to the interior can be gained from the beaches. There are no sheltered harbours in Bjornoya and vessels surprised by the weather are forced to find shelter on the lee side of the island and to anchor close in under the cliffs. In fine weather anchorage may be obtained anywhere round the island. Within a distance of about 2 miles offshore there are depths of from 8 fms. to 20 fms., the bottom in most places sand.

The island was discovered by the Dutch navigator William Barents in 1596 on a voyage in search of the North-east passage. He called it, in Dutch, Bear Island. Stephen Bennet, who visited it seven years later, called it Cherrie Is. after his patron Sir Francis Cherrie, and the erroneously spelt Cherry Is. still appears on some charts. Whalers and walrus hunters were busy there throughout the 17th century and in the 18th century they were mainly Russians who hunted and wintered on the island. They were succeeded by Norwegians who finally finished off any bear or walrus that were left. There are coal seams on the northern part of the island and during the First War coal was mined, work being finally abandoned in 1925. Tunheim, the mining town, had at its best a population of 250.

An island situated so far north and yet not far enough north nor quite high enough to maintain glaciers and snow fields, has the worst of both worlds and appears truly desolate. 'A wilderness of barren stones' is the Pilot's description, though in favoured spots there is some scant vegetation, saxifrages and a few grasses. The piles of whale and walrus bones littering the shores, and the graves of long-dead hunters, only emphasise the dreariness of the landscape. But teeming life still exists in the form of birds and during the breeding season the cliffs are almost covered with guillemots, little auks, kittiwakes, fulmar, and the burgomaster gull.

Turning eastwards along the north coast we soon spotted the radio masts and buildings of the weather station. An 'open bay' is the official description of Nordhamm and when we closed it at midnight, so little shelter did it seem to offer that I thought the word 'bay' might as well have been omitted. We anchored in four fathoms with an ugly looking rock reef some fifty yards astern. A weather station is on duty all round the clock. As we came in they were busy launching a boat and presently six guests crammed into the cabin to be entertained with cocoa and rum.

CHAPTER III

BEAR ISLAND AND ISFJORD

O NLY ONE OF OUR GUESTS, who proved to be the Base leader, spoke fluent English. Since so many of the Danes and Norwegians I have met over the years spoke English, this surprised me, and it is a tribute to the efficiency of their schools that few of those who did speak English had ever visited England. So strong is the assumption I now have that any Dane or Norwegian will immediately understand what is said to him in English, that those who do not are at once written off as ignorant foreigners. And this by a man who speaks only his own language and very little of that.

Having seen our guests safely away in the small hours we met them again at breakfast in their spacious and comfortable mess-room. In fact the main building with everything under the one roof, its big double-glazed windows overlooking the sea, might be described by an estate agent as a desirable sea-side residence for a man of means with a large family—lounge, dining room, fourteen bedrooms, the usual offices, own lighting and power plant, central heating throughout, shower baths and sauna, small private landing ground, own moorings, water frontage. In summer a ship calls once a week and in winter mail is dropped by air. Except, perhaps, in early spring the island is usually ice-free, while trawlers fish all the year round in the neighbouring waters. This accessibility is in striking contrast to that of another Norwegian weather station on the island of Hopen in the Barents Sea only some two hundred miles north-east of Bear Is.

We were told that there they had been troubled with Polar bears and that the Svalbard Governor's own vessel, a vessel strengthened against ice, had within the last fortnight been stopped by ice when trying to reach Hopen. Later in the summer, on our way home, I had hoped to call at Hopen but by then things were not going as planned.

In relays we made use of the showers and sauna, for in view of the open anchorage two of us had always to be on board. Had not the wind been well north of east the high cliffs immediately to the east would have afforded shelter; throughout our short stay this wind gradually increased and without Norwegian assistance we should have had a wet time ferrying off water in our small pram dinghy. As it was they organised our water supply and brought it off in their motor launch. Their cook baked ten loaves specially for us and they also gave us a quantity of eggs and paraffin. In my experience these far-flung weather stations are exceedingly generous to visitors like ourselves; no doubt partly on the account of their rarity, just as in those countries where travellers are few there is most hospitality.

Many of the numerous lakes and tarns on the island hold Arctic char, and the Base leader showed us with pride an aquarium he had built in which he was breeding them. He had also successfully incubated a guillemot egg and was having problems in feeding the voracious chick with the right food. Back on board we spent an uneasy night, a stiff breeze blowing directly on shore. Instead of hauling the dinghy on board we stupidly left it lying astern and none of us on anchor watch noticed when the painter parted. In the morning we spotted it lying on the beach beyond the rock reef not far from our stern. In this reef there was one narrow gap through which the dinghy had found its way, ending up unharmed on the shingle beach instead of breaking up on the rocks, a piece of luck that our carelessness hardly merited. After breakfast we broke out our inflatable dinghy in which Andrew and I went ashore paying out a long warp, for with the wind then blowing the row back would be strenuous. Having made our farewells at the base we carried the wooden dinghy to a corner of the beach where the breakers were most moderate and then rowed back tied in tandem, one man in each dinghy, helped by the line from *Baroque* and another line held by a shore party to keep us from being blown on to some rocks. We got under way with difficulty owing to *Baroque*'s reluctance to pay off on the seaward tack in contrast to her suicidal desire to rush towards the land. With little enough room for manoeuvre in that direction we swallowed our pride, downed the mains'l, and got clear by using the engine. A fine breeze just forward of the beam made up for the usual overcast sky and the absent sun, and at the pace we were going Bear Is. soon disappeared in the murk. At 6 p.m. the air temperature was 36° F and the sea 34° F. I added another sweater and a thicker pair of trousers.

All that night the continuing wind gave us a splendid sail, and for the first time on the voyage we scored a century, registering—on the log 117 miles from noon to noon. We ran clear of the overcast, too. By 8 a.m. we had the snows of Vestspitzbergen in sight glistening in the sun, while far to the north there was not a cloud in the sky. When Sorkapp, the southernmost point, came abeam to starboard we were in the lee of the land and quieter water. Some pack-ice had accumulated round the cape and we sailed through a line of small floes that had drifted to leeward. By this time we, too, had run into sunshine, a cloudless sky overhead and a sparkling, blue sea flecked with bits of ice. This is the sort of weather I have come to expect north of the Arctic Circle and do not always get, but for the next two months similar flawless days far outnumbered those with cloud and rain. For the past fortnight we had seen precious little sun and we now began to feel reasonably warm. That evening we had the wide Hornsund fjord abeam and greatly admired its fine peak Hornsundtind (4691 ft.), the most impressive mountain, I think, that we were to see. That night, thanks to the clear sky, we were allowed for the first time to see the sun at midnight; for us he would not be below the horizon again until the first week of August.

In the lee of the land *Baroque*'s immoderate burst of speed could not be sustained. Except for two short-lived blasts that obliged us to reef we had little enough wind in the next two days to Longyearbyen. These squally winds struck off the mouths of fjords and were no doubt caused by the funnelling effect of their mountainous shores. We met several ships, for what with colliers and cruise ships the west coast as far up as Isfjord is well frequented. One vessel closed us to speak and I regretted that the helmsman had stood on without calling me up, for we learnt later that she was the *Nordsyssel* with the Governor on board returning from a second and successful trip to Hopen. Our second day in Spitzbergen waters proved equally brilliant and the night not less so. As the Psalmist wrote: 'The night shineth as the day; the darkness and the light are both alike.' For the sake of 'One-upmanship' I took a meridian sight at midnight instead of noon. In contrast to the usual procedure of deducting the sun's altitude—in this case 10.38—one adds it to 90° and then deducts the sun's declination; so that 100.38 less the declination of 22.32 gave our latitude as 78.06, provided this excursion into higher mathematics is not at fault and has been understood. With the land close aboard and most of it identifiable this hard-won piece of knowledge was not essential, but I felt that the midnight sun was there for use as well as an ornament to be admired and wondered at.

Longyearbyen, the administrative capital of Svalbard, lies some thirty miles up Isfjord, the largest fjord of those parts, fifty-five miles in length and ten to fifteen miles wide. Hudson (1603) called it the Great Indraught and it was Poole (1610) who named it Ice Sound. In spite of the name it is usually ice-free from June to November and is not completely frozen over until the end of December. The flat-topped hills of the southern side, with not a glacier to be seen, are in sharp contrast with the high, serrated rock ridges to the north, ridges that are separated by large glaciers which reach right down to the waters of the fjord. Longyearbyen itself lies in Adventfjord, a short arm of the main fjord on the southern side. On 7th July, after beating into Adventfjord, when we started the engine it chose that critical moment to go hay-wire, emitting clouds of white smoke. The small jetty was already overcrowded by the two vessels lying there, *Nordsyssel* and a Russian tug. So we shaped to anchor close off the jetty and had time for only one cast of the lead before coming gently to rest on the bottom. As we discovered the engine had no power in reverse, indeed by now it had no power at all. It was about low water so we adjourned for lunch, declining the kind offer of the Russian tug to pull us off.

We were boarded by an electrician from the coalmine, a man who had plenty to say and no complaints about life in Longyearbyen— good pay, no taxes, and no temptations to riotous living. In these querulous days it is encouraging to meet anyone without a grouse or a grudge. Among other interesting things he pointed out to us a small boat used by two enterprising Norwegians for collecting driftwood logs which they cut up into saleable timber. When we were afloat again, his dinghy with its outboard together with our long sweeps were enough to move *Baroque* to the other side of the jetty where we anchored in two fathoms. It is all shallow and not good holding ground; during our stay we seemed to be either sitting on the bottom or dragging. The halcyon weather of the last few days had momentarily ended and under a lowering sky the beach of black sand where we used to land, strewn with lumps of coal, old rope, and other rubbish, wore a forlorn look. Overhead a cable-way carried coal in great buckets to the coal wharf a mile to the west.

On a wet day even the Garden of Eden may have looked sad and Longyearbyen, whose very name suggests length and dreariness, is no garden. The drizzle that set in next day merely deepened its gloom. Near the jetty are a store, the power station, and engineering shops; on the hill above are the Governor's house and the church; from there one walks nearly a mile up a bleak, barren valley flanked by abandoned mine workings to reach the township proper, comprising the Post Office, a shop, the Coal Company's offices, and the houses of its employees. A small glacier at the valley head is a cheering sight. Attached to the Post Office is a sort of lounge and coffee bar where one may relax, if that is the word, and let the busy tide of Longyearbyen roll by. I noticed outside almost every house one or more 'skidoos', a Canadian contraption for motoring on ice. In winter, I believe, they have skidoo races.

Nobody in Longyearbyen walked and none of the vehicles that sped along the road between the harbour and the township ever offered us a lift. We probably rated as tourists. On this wet day it must have been the coal dust from the overhead cableway that turned the mud at the roadside black, and the black footmarks that we left on the immaculate floor of the bakery earned us a severe rebuke from the baker. Buying bread involved paper-work and a lot of walking. The baker's bill had to be taken to the Company's office and paid, and then armed with the receipt one walked back to the bakery to collect the bread. I had a talk with the friendly Governor who put in a word on our behalf to the manager of the Coal Company which in effect runs Longyearbyen. We were allowed to buy what we needed at the Company store and they put at our disposal a diesel engine mechanic.

Paul had been wrestling with the engine ever since we arrived and had to confess himself baffled. Hence the calling in of the mechanic who after spending eight hours on the job could only suggest that we might need a new injector pump. Since the part would have to be ordered from Norway and brought out this did not help very much. Nevertheless, for his eight hours work the Company, having their shareholders to consider, billed me for £52. This exorbitant sum shook me and outraged Paul's frugal Yorkshire instincts so much that he immediately set to work again on the engine, discovered at last that the timing was at fault, and soon had it running perfectly. Although we had got nothing for our money the bill had to be paid in full, the Company insisting on the cash and not caring who got the credit. Meantime, at the end of our second day here David was missing. He had gone ashore for what was to be two hours and had not returned.

On the whole it had been a trying day but I see from my diary that Andrew and I sat up till midnight playing chess. Before leaving we had been unable to find a sea-going chess set—one in which the pieces will stay on a moving board—so Andrew set to work with his penknife and by this time had finished a set of hand-carved pieces complete with pegs at the base to fit into the handsome board that Alan made. The chessmen finished, Andrew had tried his hand at ships in bottles, while Paul, not to be outdone, started carving seals and polar bears.

At midnight we all turned in and for the first and last time set no anchor watch in the belief that we were securely anchored. It was a disturbed night. At 1 a.m. David announced his arrival on the beach and having been brought off fell into the water while climbing on board. Alan, roused by the commotion, went to help Paul who was having trouble fishing out David, for it is no easy matter hauling up a more or less inanimate body. I was on deck myself at 3 a.m. when all seemed well, but half an hour later there was bump and we found ourselves alongside a small vessel anchored much further out. Veering all the cable we had we dropped clear astern of her and then found that our cable was foul of her anchor. The two men on board whose sleep we had disturbed proved to be remarkably good-natured. Instead of venting a torrent of Norwegian Billingsgate they calmly made their appreciation, as the military say, got their anchor up, freed our cable, and anchored themselves again further away from the enemy.

David's long search for an escape from *Baroque* or an alternative means of getting home had failed, as inevitably it must in a place like

Longyearbyen, especially if the searcher is without money. Consequently he was in a morose, unhappy mood, and most unwilling to
face the inevitable. He had not yet attained to Lord Curzon's lofty phi-
losophy: 'It is inevitable, therefore it can be approved'. But once we
had left Longyearbyen, when with a little wishful thinking one could
say that we were homeward-bound, he pulled himself together, cast
care aside, and worked in the galley with zest and great success, running it more or less like clockwork with fewer and fewer calls upon
Andrew to do some winding. Meantime he had something to occupy
his mind in the matter of getting his clothes dried which he managed
by having them steamed at the power station.

Paul, with the engine now going to his satisfaction, took a day
off to go fossicking among the old mine workings. Industrial archaeology, he called it, and together with Alan triumphantly brought
back some old miner's lamps which they lovingly cleaned and polished. All was grist to their mill. Besides lamps they had a pair of
boots—miner's boots presumably—reindeer horns, and the skull of
an Arctic fox, or maybe a domestic dog. As mementoes of Svalbard,
for they had started collecting them at Bear Island, bones were highly
prized by all the crew, bones of whales, seals, bears, and, of course,
reindeer horns. Later on, at more than one anchorage, where there
were the graves of old-time whaling men and trappers, I admired
their restraint in not digging up a skeleton or two for their collection.
These relics were not really welcome in the cabin, so we had a large
box for them on deck.

We waited until 12th July in order to collect some expected mail
and early that morning the cruise ship Regina Magna came in. Hundreds of tourists, Europeans, or at any rate middle-Europeans, disem-
barked to proceed by bus and taxi to the Post Office and the shop. A
few of the hardier types preferred to walk and these became the prey of
some enterprising Norwegian boys who had set up a stall by the roadside for the sale of fossils. Vestspitzbergen is rich in fossils.

Among the stores that we had bought were twenty-four loaves
of white bread and it was the nature of this bread that really determined our next port of call. According to Sir Fopling Flutter, 'Beyond
Hyde Park all is desert'; beyond Longyearbyen, too, all is, so to speak,
desert, it is the last place where anything can be bought. If we failed in

our circumnavigation we should, of course, have to return by the west
coast, but if we succeeded I intended going directly home (after a call
at Hopen) and this implied starting from Longyearbyen with stores,
including bread, for two months. The only kind of bread that would
keep that long without going mouldy is black bread, readily obtainable in Greenland, for instance, under the name of 'rugbrod'. It has
the additional advantage of becoming harder with age so that as time
goes on the crew eat less and less. None of this could be had at Longyearbyen but I readily assumed that Russians would eat nothing else,
despising anything so cissy as white bread. The Russian mining town
of Barentsburg was therefore to be our next stop.

The Russians lease two mines at Isfjord, one at Pyramiden at the
head of the fjord and another at Barentsburg in Greenfjord on the same
side of Isfjord as Longyearbyen and close to the entrance. Compared
with most coal mines those in Vestspitzbergen are easy to work. The
seams lie high up on the hillside so that instead of deep shafts having
to be sunk they can be reached by adits driven in at the same level;
moreover the mines are close to the sea and the coal goes direct from
the mine to the ship's hold—in the case of Longyearbyen by a cable
conveyor two and a half miles in length. Finally owing to the frozen
soil there are no water problems and little need for pit props.

Thanks to a fresh northerly breeze, by supper time we were
off the Greenfjord entrance where we gybed and sailed in. Inside
the wind died away, thus frustrating our hope of astonishing the
natives by approaching the town under sail. Why the fjord was
named Green Harbour by Poole in 1610 is not immediately obvious,
unless it was because there are no glaciers in sight. Three ships lay
at anchor waiting to load and one lay alongside a small jetty having
coal poured into her in rather slow time. Unlike Longyearbyen the
town is compact, all the buildings, badly in need of paint, huddled
together a few hundred feet above the jetty. Three helicopters were
parked nearby. Having cruised up and down and found no obvious
anchorage for small craft we decided to anchor off a little bit of
beach just ahead of the vessel coaling. By then (10 p.m.) a crowd of
curious sightseers had gathered on the beach, many of them armed
with cameras. Close in the water shoaled abruptly to three fathoms.
Going hard astern had no effect—we should have remembered—so

that we slid gently to rest on the mud almost eyeball to eyeball with the nearest Russian.

One could almost have waded, but I rowed ashore and presently got into conversation with one of the reception party. Conversation, implying two-way traffic, is hardly the word. While my new-found friend volleyed away in fluent German, the only words in that language that I could summon up were 'schwarzbrod' and 'funfzehn'.

Apparently he got the message. It was too late then, but early next morning we should have our fifteen loaves of black bread. Meantime a kindly bystander, catching at least part of the message, rushed off and returned with four white loaves for which he firmly refused the proffered cigarettes.

Back on board we had a visitor, a young Norwegian working for a Norwegian company who were laying a pipe-line across Greenfjord to augment Barentsburg's water supply. He messed with the Russians and found it distressing—beans for the most part and liberal quantities of poor quality margarine with everything. Instead of beer, which was not to be had, they got a ration of two bottles of Vodka a month, and should we happen to have on board a copy of *Playboy* we could swop it for three bottles of Vodka. He confirmed what one would suspect, namely that Russia is not so destitute of coal deposits that they have to be eked out with Spitzbergen coal, and that the leasing of the mines there is more for the sake of maintaining a foothold.

Early next morning before anyone was about I went ashore again for a quick look round. The only way of getting from sea level to the town above, apart from the coal chute, seemed to be by way of a long flight of wooden steps. This possibly accounted for the mass of material piled anyhow on the beach almost down to tidemark—iron pipes by the mile, steel joists, cement, timber, drums of cable, coils of wire. Except for the absence of warlike stores it might have been a badly organised war-time beach-head. Half-way up the steps was a mammoth greenhouse crammed with plants which I could not identify from outside. The door was locked. In this they were one-up on Longyearbyen though the produce from a single greenhouse would not go far among the thousand or more inhabitants of Barentsburg.

When the whistle blew and work started our beach remained singularly empty. No one came near it. Copies of *Playboy* would have found no takers, trade and barter had ceased, the Iron Curtain lowered and the Cold War resumed. Word must have gone around that fraternising with yacht-owning, capitalist lackeys must cease. All cameras had been put away or confiscated. Hours passed and no one came near the beach or so much as looked at us. We had already kedged ourselves off the mud, so when noon came and found us still, as it were, in quarantine, we got our anchor and sailed for the north. So much for Russian black bread.

CHAPTER IV

TO THE MOUNTAINS

A NOTED FEATURE ON THE WEST COAST is Prins Karls Forland, a long, narrow island lying parallel to the coast and separated from it by a channel known as Forlandsundet. The island, nearly fifty miles in length, is well furnished with mountains and glaciers, the highest mountain rising to 3500 ft. The southern entrance to Forlandsundet is just off Isfjord and its northern exit is off Kongsfjord whither we were then bound. Conveniently enough, therefore, we could make the whole passage in the quiet waters of Forlandsundet. A bar runs right across the sound over which the greatest depth is 13 ft. Ships of any size are therefore obliged to pass outside.

In discussing the naming of Prins Karls Forland the *Arctic Pilot* reveals in its laconic way something that would surprise or even startle a student of mountaineering history:

> It was named Prince Charles Island by Fotherby (1616) after the son of James 1st, who afterwards reigned as Charles 1st, while at the same time it was known to Dutch whalers as Kijn Island, after a super-cargo who broke his neck while climbing a mountain on the island.

Where in a matter such as this one's curiosity is never likely to be satisfied, it is maddening to have it aroused by the throw-away remark 'broke his neck while climbing' as if climbing in Spitzbergen early in the 17th century was a normal activity, and that Dutch whaling men, of all people, took part in it. De Saussure's ascent of Mt. Blanc in 1787 is generally accepted as marking the beginning of mountaineering as a sport, although his motives were not altogether pure as they were a little tainted by science. Thus to learn that De Saussure's historic initiative had been anticipated by a hundred and fifty years or more is like discovering that cricket matches were played every Saturday afternoon in, say, Paris, long before they thought of it at Hambledon.

Much depends upon what poor Kijn's motives for climbing were and that we shall never know. It is more than likely that he was not climbing for fun but on business, looking for whales or surveying ice conditions from some lofty look-out, and since we know neither this nor what mountain he was climbing, any claim to regard him as the father of mountaineering instead of De Saussure would be difficult to establish. To have one's name recorded in the *Arctic Pilot* is surely a kind of immortality and with that Kijn, Dutch supercargo and embryo mountaineer, will have to be content.

Before we had quite cleared the Isfjord entrance we were struck by another of those furious, short-lived blasts of wind blowing out of the fjord. For the two hours it lasted we dropped the stays'l and reefed down. Once inside Forlandsundet we had little enough wind while a steady drizzle so reduced visibility that the mountains on the Forland remained hidden. Thus when approaching the bar we were not as confident as we should have been to our whereabouts or of hitting off the channel. This channel, with a least depth of two fathoms, is half a mile long and only a cable and a bit wide. It is indicated by a pecked line on the chart and the point of departure for it on the Forland side is marked by a beacon which we failed to see. The least depth we got with the lead was four fathoms, but I suspect that by then the bar had long been crossed.

The ten-mile wide entrance to Kongsfjord is marked on the north side by a prominent peak called The Mitre, an apt name for once since it is cleft down the middle and when viewed from the south does resemble a bishop's mitre. It was so named by William Scoresby of Scoresby Sound fame, whaling captain, explorer, scientist, and finally Church of England parson, an all-rounder, man of action and man of intellect, the sort that is not bred nowadays. He not only named the Mitre but climbed both it and a neighbouring summit, finding the ridge between the two so sharp that he traversed it *à cheval*, a leg on either side. Scoresby's *Account of the Arctic Regions*, first published in 1820, is in two volumes, one dealing very thoroughly with whaling while the other, besides scientific matter, includes a general account of the west coast of Vestspitzbergen in which his ascent of Mitre peak, a modest 1233 ft., is graphically described. Scoresby spent twenty-five years voyaging in Arctic waters, going to sea first at the age of fourteen in his father's whaling ship *Resolution*, and when writing of ships and the sea, the element whereon he was supreme, his style is severe, sober, seaman-like; but the rarified atmosphere of Mitre peak goes to his head and he becomes exuberant, almost intoxicated:

> The prospect was most extensive and grand, mountain rising above mountain until by distance they dwindled into insignificancy; the whole contrasted by a canopy of deepest azure, and enlightened by the rays of a blazing sun, and the effect marked by a feeling of danger, seated as we were on a pinnacle of rock almost surrounded by tremendous precipices, all united to constitute a picture singularly sublime. Here we seemed elevated to the very heavens, and though in an hazardous situation, I was sensible only of pleasing emotions, heightened by the persuasion that, from experience in these adventures I was superior to the dangers with which I was surrounded… The effect of the elevation and the brightness of the picture were such that the sea, which was at least a league from us, appeared within reach of a musket shot, mountains a dozen miles off, seemed scarcely a league from us, and our vessel, which we knew to be a league from the shore, appeared in danger of the rocks.

The ascent had been difficult enough, for as well as the *mauvais pas*, already mentioned, which they overcame by sitting astride, the loose-ness of the terrain had reduced them to more unorthodox methods, methods which no mountaineer would think of copying even when climbing a sandhill, and which the Alpine Club, had it then existed, would have certainly sneered at: '…the ground gave way at every step and no progress was made; hence the only method of succeeding was by the effort of leaping and running, which under the circumstances could not be accomplished without excessive fatigue'. The descent, naturally, was worse: 'We found it really a very hazardous and in some instances a painful undertaking. The way now seemed precipitous. Every movement was a work of deliberation.' But Scoresby had in him the makings of a mountaineer, recognising at once the dangers implicit in descending loose rock and as readily hitting on a way of obviat-ing the danger; 'We were careful to advance abreast of each other, for any individual being below us would have been in danger of being overwhelmed with the stones which we unintentionally dislodged in showers.' On this perilous Mitre peak adventure Scoresby does not seem to have taken the precaution which Martens, an earlier Spitzbergen explorer to whom he refers, deemed essential: 'The necessity,' writes Martens, 'of marking every step with chalk, as the adventurer climbs the rugged mountain, otherwise he will not know how to get down.' Frederick Martens' book, *A Voyage to Spitzbergen*, describes a voyage undertaken in 1671.

From Mitre Peak which started this long digression, it is time to return to Kongsfjord where we, too, hoped to do some climbing. I might add that in spite of Scoresby the Mitre did not seem worth a second ascent—devoid of snow or ice and probably what Baedeker would have written off as 'fatiguing and not repaying'. We also wanted to visit Ny Alesund, a place that formerly had been of some importance. The coal mines there had been abandoned but in 1937 the Norwegian Government converted most of the buildings into the North Pole Hotel and Ny Alesund blossomed as a short-lived tourist centre. Nowadays hotels are built in even more unlikely places. In 1950, the first party from the outside world ever to visit Thyangboche on the Nepal side of Mt. Everest (Dr. Charles Houston and his father, Mrs. Betsy Cowles, Anderson Bakewell S.J., and the present writer) little imagined that in less than twenty-five years so remote a spot, sanctified by a Bhuddist monastery, would become a tourist centre complete with hotel.

Kongsfjord trends south-east and Ny Alesund lies on the south side some ten miles in. There are no hazards in the approach and on 16th July, a lovely, warm day, we anchored close to the small jetty. On a little peninsula opposite Ny Alesund there is a place with a familiar name, London; it is the site of a disused marble quarry and unlike its greater rival has now only one house. On this sunny day, if one ignored an overpowering concrete structure as high as a sky-scraper and as windowless as a pill-box, Ny Alesund with its mountain background wore a far more cheering aspect than either Longyearbyen or Barentsburg. The North Pole Hotel is, of course, no more so there were no brightly garbed Americans sunning themselves on the jetty, but I did have one pleasing encounter when I first went ashore. In the shadow of the giant pill-box a Land Rover passed, stopped, and the Norwegian driver hailed me by name. To my shame I failed to recognise him, for he proved to be the man who had been Commandant of the Norwegian station at Jan Mayen in '68 when we had to beach *Mischief* there and subsequently lost her. He was now in charge at Ny Alesund and had the ungrateful task of closing the station or at least running it down. Besides an air-strip and a weather station there was a European satellite tracking station with the familiar monster plastic dome housing the sensitive antennae. Of these only the weather station and the power plant necessary for lighting and heating were to remain. Ny Alesund has had nothing but setbacks. The hotel did not survive the war and long before that the coalmine had been closed down as the result of an explosion that killed a number of miners. We visited the old workings where even now the evidence of violent destruction, pieces of buildings and machinery strewn far and wide, is sufficiently striking.

My Jan Mayen friend drove me into the town where, in what might be called the High Street, he introduced me to Professor Harland, an old Spitzbergen hand, who was then in charge of a geological party of twenty from the Sedgewick Museum, Cambridge. Even in Lat. 79° N. such a fine, wide street as this deserved to be lined with something. Plane trees, of course, were out, lamp-posts were superfluous because of the absence of night, so instead they had lined it with Huskies' kennels, a dozen each side; ingenious kennels made from those great wooden drums on which cable is wound, the hub part with a door cut in it forming a commodious dog's home. Outside each, on a chain, sat the proud owner.

The Cambridge party were widely scattered while the Professor himself and several others were about to leave for the north coast in their two small cabin cruisers. By chance we met them there later. There are many empty houses in Ny Alesund and the building they were occupying may well have been part of the old hotel. No doubt they were drier but compared with us they seemed to be having a hard time, living entirely on pre-packed twelve-man-day ration boxes. Consequently ever since their arrival in Spitzbergen they had not eaten bread or even any of the simpler flour products such as soda bread or chapatties. When the Professor, together with the Naval officer who was in charge of their boats, and a geological student, later visited us at tea-time they regarded our bread and butter as a rare treat. There is something to be said for pre-packed ration boxes in that they save the men in the field a lot of trouble, the trouble of having to think, to improvise, or to cook, and at the same time they must convince those same men that they are indeed on an expedition. To eke out our bread and flour we needed some biscuit so we did a swop with the Cambridge party—ten boxes of Lifeboat biscuit and a ration box in exchange for some flour, dried egg, and potatoes. Lifeboat biscuits are part of the emergency food carried in ship's lifeboats. On the longer voyages in *Mischief* I used to carry a lot of them and even in those days they were not cheap, 12/- (old shillings) for a box of forty-eight small biscuits. The small size is a point in their favour, for on them it is not possible to convey to the mouth unduly large quantities of butter and jam. A Norwegian whose own plans had come unstuck also had a number of ration boxes for disposal. I felt sorry for him but not quite sorry enough to pay the price he wanted for ration boxes.

The day of our arrival Andrew succumbed to a violent attack of migraine, as he did on more than one occasion later. In the matter of illness or accidents on the part of the crew all these voyages have been lucky; only twice have men had to be landed, one with a threatened appendicitis and the other with a tooth abscess, and each time we were reasonably close to a port. Paul, Alan, and I went to look at the old mine workings and, of greater interest, the *Italia* mooring mast and the Amundsen memorial. On the 23rd May 1928 the airship *Italia*, designed and commanded by Gen. Nobile, set out from Ny Alesund to fly to the North Pole. Three years earlier in the airship *Norge*, accompanied by Amundsen and Ellsworth, he had flown over the Pole to Nome in Alaska. In 1928 the *Italia* reached the Pole but on the return flight bad weather and other troubles forced Nobile to make a crash-landing off the coast of Northeastland. Only the cabin and its ten occupants, Nobile with a broken leg, survived the landing, the body of the airship together with the gondola and six men in it being blown away by the wind never to be seen again. The cabin party had ample food and the wireless set still worked. Every hour they sent out an S.O.S. signal but their support ship at Barentsburg in Greenfjord was not listening. By chance a Russian amateur picked up the signal and a rescue on an international scale was speedily mounted. Amundsen, in spite of having quarrelled bitterly with Nobile over the conduct of the Norge expedition, was one of the first to respond and in so doing lost

his life, his plane with two French pilots disappearing on the way to
Spitzbergen. A Swedish airman finally located the wrecked cabin and
brought back Nobile. On his second attempt, however, his plane over-
turned alongside the cabin and the task of rescuing the whole party,
including two men who had walked ashore to Northeastland to seek
help, was finally accomplished by a Russian ice-breaker. The stone
memorial, suitably inscribed in Italian, commemorates Amundsen's
heroic end, in keeping with the life of that most illustrious explorer.
On one of *Mischief*'s voyages I saw on South Georgia the memorial to
another great explorer, Shackleton, who died at sea off South Georgia
in 1922. Perhaps men of such achievements need no memorials but at
Ny Alesund and even more in the grimmer surroundings of Grytviken
I found them moving. Contemplating the ruins of Iona Dr. Johnson
wrote:

> To abstract the mind from all local emotion would be impossible if it
> were endeavoured, and would be foolish if it were possible. Whatever
> withdraws us from the power of our senses; whatever makes the past,
> the distant, or the future predominate over the present, advances us
> in the dignity of thinking beings.

The gloriously fine weather continuing, Paul and Alan set off for a
long ridge climb taking with them an assortment of ironmongery. This
remained unused, for the rock, both here and elsewhere, proved to be
almost uniformly soft and rotten, nowhere to be trusted, and on the
whole unsuitable either for free or artificial climbing. A small peak
much closer at hand attracted me. It was mainly snow and I had no
axe, so I picked up a stake at the old mine workings and fashioned it
into a shortened form of alpenstock. Two hours up and one down sufficed which meant that it cannot have been more than 2000 ft. The only
hazards of this expedition were encountered on the approach march
through what might be called the suburbs of Ny Alesund where Arctic
terns, nesting by the roadside, made it their business to attack anyone
on foot. They did not often press their attack home, usually pulling
out of their dive before actually striking, but twice I received taps on
the head. My alpenstock, flourished continuously like a bandmaster's
staff, helped to keep them at bay.

Mollerfjord anchorage, Spitzbergen

Having seen all the sights, climbed two peaks, and put in some industrial archaeology at the old mine, we were ready to go. The *Nordsyssel* came in and occupied the jetty and after she had left we went alongside to fill up with oil and water. When we sailed on 18th July we had not far to go. Krossfjord, where we intended spending a few days, is merely a northern extension of Kongsfjord. It is well provided with mountains and at the head of its main branch is a popular tourist ship attraction, what the Pilot calls the 'immense glacier of Lilliehook'. If compared with some Himalayan or Greenland glaciers its immensity shrinks considerably. As the Red Queen said: 'I have seen hills compared with which these are valleys'. Icebergs, of course, are calved from glaciers, yet all the numerous glaciers of Vestspitzbergen between them produce nothing really worthy of the name. Anyone accustomed to Greenland waters where vast and slightly less vast icebergs are nearly always in sight, their diversity of shape, size, and colour a constant source of delight, will regret the absence of anything comparable around Vestspitzbergen. The glaciers are on a much smaller scale than those from which the Greenland bergs are calved, for these are fed by and descend from the great ice-sheet thousands of feet thick that covers most of the interior. With reference to the Lilliehook glacier the Pilot has this to say of bergs:

> From this glacier large bergs are frequently calved, many with a height of 40 to 50 ft. and a length and breadth of over half a mile. These are the only real icebergs calved on the west coast, for the masses of ice that break off from the considerable glaciers in the fjords are very much smaller. The reason for the larger size of the Lilliehook calvings appears to be the greater depth of water at the front of the glacier. None of the Lilliehook bergs, however, appear to reach the open sea, as having too great a draught, they ground either on the banks fringing the fjord or on the shoals near the entrance. Small vessels should keep well clear of the front of the Lilliehook glacier as it calves frequently, and the waves then raised are sufficiently high to be dangerous for a considerable distance.

It is not only the west coast that is devoid of sizeable icebergs, for neither on the north coast nor the east did we encounter any. Towards the head of Krossfjord there were a few floes and one miniature berg drifting about and I concluded that if we anchored there these were likely to prove a nuisance. There is another branch fjord that trends away to the north-east and since from the chart we could see that the glacier at its head did not reach the water there would be no floes there to bother us. The anchorage, too, was said to be good, so thither we went.

While proceeding up Krossfjord on the way to this other branch which is called Mollerfjord, we made out the cruise ship *Regina Maris* right up near the front of the Lilliehook glacier, the captain evidently doing his best to give his passengers their money's worth. Near the head of Mollerfjord on the east shore, a conspicuous boulder some twenty feet high makes a useful leading mark for the anchorage. On inspection its face proved to be fairly smooth and I mentioned this to the crew, as well as the fact that Darius, the great king, liked to have his victories and progressions commemorated upon any convenient rock face—at Bisitun near Kermanshah, for example. Paul and Andrew between them could no doubt have carved an elaborate inscription had we had time to spare. On the other hand we had plenty of paint.

In the morning I had myself rowed across to the west shore, a longish row, where a good looking peak of about my low standard challenged attention. Having ascended the south side by way of a convenient snow gully I descended the north side by a much steeper gully, steep enough in its upper part to oblige me to face inwards to kick steps, using the hands for support. The dinghy had been taken back so I walked round the head of the fjord, an estuary of mud flats and innumerable small streams left behind by the retreating glacier. Back by the conspicuous boulder I found Paul already hard at work with a paint brush and making a good job of it with the name *Baroque* and the date extending right across the face. Unfortunately this will not endure as long as the rock-carvings at Bisitun and whether in the future there will be the opportunity to touch it up is more than doubtful; in 1973 we were able to touch up the *Mischief* we had painted on the rock wall overlooking Godthaab harbour in 1963. Commemorative vandalism, as this might be called, recording one's name and date of visit, preferably in indelible pencil, is a weakness that tourists and trippers suffer from, particularly the British variety. But recording the name and date of a ship's visit to a remote place is, perhaps, more excusable and personally I enjoyed scanning the names painted on the wall at God-thaab, guessing at the various nationalities and even recognising the names of ships that one had met or passed.

Along the shores of Vestspitzbergen fjords huts or the remains of huts are a fairly common sight, the relics of Norwegian and Russian hunters of bygone days or of past expeditions. A hut half a mile from the big boulder seemed to be an objective for cruise ships and to be maintained by them in good order—shovels and brushes for clearing out snow, a stove and fuel, a stock of tinned food, a visitor's book, and a home-made chess set—the last item, in my opinion, not nearly so good as Andrew's. The visitor's book, which we took the liberty of signing, contained the names of hundreds of tourists, most of them German off the cruise ship *Europa*.

The most challenging peak within reach lay to the south on the far side of an arm of Mollerfjord at the head of which was a terribly broken glacier. The easiest approach was by water, thus avoiding the crossing of the glacier, so Paul and Alan got Andrew to row them across, a journey that took a good hour. The fog that had prevailed had lifted but above the 500 ft. level thick clouds writhed around all the peaks, at times concealing and again revealing unexpected features in a way that baffled the beholder:

> The hills are shadows and they flow
> From form to form and nothing stands,
> They melt like mists; the solid lands
> Like clouds they shape themselves and go.

As might be expected the climbers could make nothing of it. They spent the day groping, knowing neither where they were nor where their peak lay. They did not get back until 9 p.m. by when the clouds had dispersed and all lay revealed. Even so they could not point out with any certainty on which of several buttresses they had spent an unrewarding day.

On the 21st, fine but windless, we waited for the tide to drift us down to Krossfjord where we expected to find some wind. In the fjord we passed yet another cruise ship, the French line *Renaissance*, and by evening were approaching the entrance with C. Mitre abeam. Both the chart and the Pilot warn the mariner of foul ground near the cape and although we were a good two miles off we saw close ahead white water breaking over a sunken rock. Without either our modern charts or pilotage directions, in unhandy ships, the Dutch and English whaling men of the 17th century who made so free with this coast must have been superbly skilful and daring seamen. No doubt the knowledge gained bit by bit was soon pieced together and became widely diffused throughout the fleets, and the fact that they sailed in company was an advantage, for it is a comfort to know that there are other ships in the vicinity. It may be regrettable but it is certainly true that these hazards and hardships were incurred for the sake of profit and that should not lessen one's admiration for such redoubtable characters.

We were bound for Magdalena fjord about twenty-five miles further north and in the course of an almost windless night managed to drift a good part of the way. At breakfast time the *Renaissance* passed again bound north. She turned up again late that evening in Magdalena fjord so she may well have spent the day steaming as far north as she could, possibly as far as N. Lat. 81 where she would probably be able to astonish her passengers by having the Polar pack in sight. Magdalena fjord runs east-north-eastwards and has at its head the 300 ft. high ice front of the Waggonway glacier, at least a mile in width, rivalling as a tourist attraction the great Lilliehook glacier. This fjord, reputedly the most beautiful of Vestspitzbergen fjords, was visited first by Barents in 1596 who named it Tusk Bay from the finding of two walrus tusks. Fotherby in 1616 called it Maudlen Sound and the anchorage at its head Trinitie Harbour, which is now the Trinityhamna where we anchored that evening. Sailors are said to be conservative folk and accordingly the editor of the 1961 edition of the *Arctic Pilot* has based much of the description of Magdalena fjord upon a report by Lieut. Beechey who visited the fjord in H.M.S. *Trent* in 1818. Since 1818 there have, of course, been other visitors to Magdalena—there were several hundred there that evening—some of whom could have made a concise and up-to-date report for the Pilot; but despite the inevitable inaccuracies, I for one applaud the preference given to Lieut. Beechey, for he must be the same Lieut. Beechey who was on Parry's expedition in search of the North-west passage in 1829, still a lieutenant eleven years later, promotion no doubt being damnably slow in the piping days of peace subsequent to the Napoleonic war. A figure from the heroic days

Magdalena fjord with Waggonway glacier in the background; Paul is at the tiller

of Arctic exploration deserves to be thus remembered in the *Arctic Pilot* even if his observations no longer hold good.

A glaring example of this is the description of a glacier called Hangebreen not far from Trinityhamna:

> Hangebreen, or Hanging Glacier, though the smallest in size, is the most remarkable of the glaciers visible. It is situated at an elevation of about 200 ft. on the slopes of a mountain, in such an apparently precarious position that it looks as if a slight shock would precipitate it into the sea. Large portions do occasionally break away and fall down the mountain side, making this part of the fjord hazardous to approach in a small boat.

Since 1818 this little glacier has retreated so far from the water, diminished so much in size, and lies at such a gentle angle that it is hard to imagine any ice breaking off let alone reaching the water.

Still relying upon Lieut. Beechey, attention is drawn to a striking contrast between the north and south sides of the fjord, the latter, on account of the steep mountains, seldom if ever being visited by the sun. Accordingly we read:

> While on the southern side perpetual frost is converting into ice the streams of water occasioned by the thawing snow on those upper parts of the mountains which are exposed to the sun's rays, the northern shore is relieving itself of its superficial winter crust and refreshing a vigorous vegetation with its moisture.

On my reading this, averse as ever to avoidable hardship, I seriously thought of foregoing the well-known, secure anchorage of Trinityhamna and instead seeking an anchorage on the verdant, sun-bathed north shore. Yet, in July, both sides of the fjord appeared to be equally barren, the sun occasionally lit on Trinityhamna, and there was never any question of freezing, the numerous small streams running merrily night and day. Finally, for good measure, the Pilot adds: 'Landing is difficult anywhere in Magdalena fjord', whereas at Trinityhamna nothing could be easier, the *Renaissance*, as we shall see, landing several hundred people that night.

With reason, mariners regard the Admiralty Pilots much as one would Holy Writ. Nevertheless, although attempts to bring the Bible up to date are to be deplored this should not apply to them. As there are some seventy volumes the mere keeping of them up-to-date is a sufficiently formidable task, and since the three volumes of the *Arctic Pilot* cannot be in great demand they probably have a low priority. On the whole, in the matter of Magdalena fjord and Lieut. Beechey, it is better to be harmlessly misinformed than that his name should be forgotten.

As mentioned above the *Renaissance* came in that evening and we were able to witness a cruise ship in action, as it were. She anchored just outside Trinityhamna and although it had begun to rain smartly preparations began for giving her passengers a run ashore. A pontoon was positioned near the sandy beach of Trinityhamna and a gangway rigged from the pontoon to the shore, after which two or three big launches, each holding about fifty people, maintained a shuttle service from ship to shore. This went on until midnight. Pontoon and gangway were then dismantled, launches and accommodation ladders hoisted on board, and at 5 a.m. she sailed. The whole business went smoothly like a familiar drill, as no doubt it was.

The sandspit where all this coming and going took place is called Graveneset. As the name implies it has on it a number of graves and a stone memorial inscribed 'Svalbardfrareri 1600–1750'. The sandspit forms a protecting arm round Trinityhamna which is a safe and pleasant anchorage, almost free from drifting floes, and with a number of peaks within striking distance. As far as I remember only one floe drifted in and that had on it a fat seal fast asleep, probably a harp seal, easy meat had we had on board a rifle and felt sufficiently brutal. 'God Almighty, what things a man sees when he is without a gun,' is a remark attributed to a Boer farmer. We had no weapons of any kind and the crew's respect for life would have profoundly shocked men like Lamont and Leigh Smith, wealthy Victorian yachtsmen whose passion for slaughter, particularly the slaughtering of walrus, Polar bears, and seals, led them to sailing in Arctic waters.

The next day, fine but dull, the climbers followed their vocation. Paul and Alan took on the two nearest peaks while I went for one more distant. The approach march involved a mile of boulder-hopping along the shore, a disagreeable pastime most often associated with

Mountains in Magdalena fjord, Spitzbergen

Himalayan glaciers and their moraines. A long glacier walk and a gradual ascent on hard névé left only a few hundred feet of steeper snow
to climb. Like most of the peaks we climbed one side fell away almost
sheer and there almost every ledge and cranny of the crumbling cliff
were the homes of countless little auks.

The next target chosen by Paul and Alan lay half-way up the Waggonway glacier, thus providing them with a long row, a long glacier
walk, and a fine, long ridge to traverse. We had noticed two tents at the
foot of the glacier and our climbers found them occupied by a party
of Norwegians and Swiss. They were at the end of their stay, due to
be picked up the following day, and already beginning to pack up.
I went for a peak on the far side of a glacier known as Gully Glacier
which descended to the water in a steep and broken ice-fall. Well above
this, where I crossed, the mile-wide glacier consisted of smooth 'dry'
ice, that is without any snow cover. The ice itself was by no means
dry in the ordinary sense, the melt-water pouring off in deep runnels.
Normally one avoids traversing a glacier alone but where there is no
snow cover, as here, the crevasses are wide open and easy to avoid or to
jump. As I began a long, slow plug up snow of variable quality I had
leisure to ponder upon the immortal lines of one Joseph Cottle, a very
minor poet:

> How steep, how painful the ascent;
> It needs the evidence of close deduction
> To know that I shall ever gain the top.

My peak was crowned with a rock tower that when viewed from afar
might have been described as beyond the bounds of human possibility. From below I had certainly written it off as beyond my bounds and
was content to forego it. As often happens, closer inspection diminished its terror and in fact it presented hardly any difficulty even to my
faltering footsteps.

Rain and thick mist on the 26th gave us an excuse for staying at
Trinityhamna instead of sailing as intended. We spent the time writing
letters with a view to handing them to the ship that was due to collect
the Norwegian-Swiss party. She came in late at night and anchored
near the Waggonway glacier a long way from us. As I had the anchor
watch I set off in the dinghy to intercept her but she got her anchor and

steamed away long before I had got within hailing distance. Having thus, as we thought, missed the post, Alan made up a mail-bag and fastened it to a pole near the Graveneset memorial, hoping that among the next shipload of tourists there would be someone curious enough to open it. No sooner had he done this than our old acquaintance *Regina Magna* came in, anchored off Gully glacier, and began landing her passengers on the far side of Graveneset. So we motored round towards her and then sent off Alan in the dinghy to hand over our mail to one of her launches. Thick fog having by now come down we went back to Trinityhamna for lunch and sailed late in the afternoon when the fog had lifted.

Readers will probably agree with me that all this tourist activity in Magdalena fjord and elsewhere, while convenient for posting letters, detracts not a little from the romance that even in these days should still cling to so distant and so desolate an island, an island where almost every name recalls the bold seamen and explorers of the past. From now on, however, we should be on our own. In a small boat on the north and east coasts of Vestspitzbergen one feels almost as far out on a limb as one could wish.

CHAPTER V

TO HINLOPEN STRAIT

◆

THE BEST TIME FOR TACKLING A PLACE like Hinlopen Strait where ice is likely to be met would probably be late in August. Rather than hang about until then—though there were still places of interest to visit—I felt an impatient urge to try our luck as soon as possible and so to have done. I had on my mind the possibility of being stopped by ice at the southern end of the strait and faced with the long haul back round the north and west coasts, no doubt feeling sour and depressed by defeat. Not that that would have been the first time by any means, or the last, that we have had to sail home empty-handed, mission unaccomplished. In Magdalena fjord, therefore, we had climbed our last mountain. Those few we had climbed were modest enough in height and the rudimentary cairns that adorned most of them proclaimed that ours were not the first ascents. But there are no guide-books for Spitzbergen mountains and for us they were as good as virgin peaks up and down which we had to find our own way. On that account alone they had given us a lot of pleasure and had been well worth a visit.

After so many days in sheltered waters we had now to put to sea and on quitting the fjord we were soon reminded of such things as waves. A fresh head wind obliged us to reef down and raised such a short, steep sea that both Paul and David were temporarily overcome. Once more they had to find their sea-legs. The direction of the wind, too, discouraged us from trying a slightly shorter way to the north coast through Smeerenburg fjord inside Danes Is. and Amsterdam Is. These names remind one that this north-west corner of Vestspitzbergen which we were now rounding was more frequented by the whaling ships of the 17th century than any other part. At the height of the whaling industry of those days so much quarrelling and even fighting arose among the ships of the several nations engaged that finally an agreement was made to apportion the various harbours. Hence English Bay on Prins Karls Forland, for example, while Danes Is. and Amsterdam

Is. were Danish and Dutch preserves. The expressive name of Smeerenburg, or Blubber town, the harbour on Amsterdam Is., speaks for
itself. In its palmiest days between 1633 and 1643 Smeerenburg had
1200 inhabitants, besides the crews of a hundred or more whalers lying
in the bay. The Spaniards, French, and Hamburgers, as they were the
weaker parties, had to be content with such harbours that the bully-
boys of those days—the English and the Dutch—did not want. All of
them, however, English and Dutch included, were indebted to or relied
upon Biscayners, who from long experience of whaling off their own
coast were employed throughout the fleets in the essential roles of har-
pooners and coopers.

Danes Is. is noteworthy on another account. It was from here
that on 11th July 1897 Andrée embarked on his ill-fated balloon flight
towards the North Pole. Nothing more was seen or heard of Andrée
and his party for the next thirty years and only by the merest chance
did the tragic ending to the flight become known. In 1930 a Norwegian sealer happened to anchor off White Is., a small island to the east
of Northeastland. On going ashore they found the remains of a camp
and the bodies of Andrée and his companions Strindberg and Fraen-
kel, and in the pocket of Andrée's coat, his diary. The flight had lasted
for sixty-five hours before the balloon came down on the ice having
made good some 350 miles to the north-east. In the colder air over the
pack-ice the gas had contracted and although they threw out ballast
and everything they could spare they could not keep the balloon aloft.

When the party fetched White Is. on the 5th October they had
with them enough bear and seal meat to last them through the winter.
There Andrée's diary ends but Strindberg wrote some notes until on
17th Oct. he died and was buried by the two survivors. How long
after that they survived is not known. Various conjectures have been
made as to why, with apparently ample food, they should all have
succumbed—poisoned by eating bear liver or suffocated with fumes
from their stove? Nansen and Johansen, when they left the *Fram* on
her Polar drift, had been travelling over the ice for five months before
they reached Franz Josef islands where they wintered successfully in
similar hard or harder conditions, living on bear meat. Nansen, however, was an experienced Polar traveller and when reading the Andrée
diaries some time ago I had the impression that he and his men started

out poorly clad to withstand an Arctic winter, lacked the know-how to improvise, and may have died from cold and exhaustion. Hakluyt's Headland, a bold, 1000 ft. high granite cliff on Amsterdam Is. marks the north-western extremity of Vestspitzbergen. After passing this we continued north and for another thirty miles to reach 80° 04′ N. our furthest north, on 28th July. The sun slowly burnt up the sullen fog that lay in patches all round the horizon and by noon it shone from a cloudless sky upon a calm, unblemished sea. In the distant south the land lay glistening white and to the north open water, no ice anywhere in sight. The sight reminded me of words used by the great Elizabethan seaman-explorer John Davis when in 1587 he reached his furthest north off the cape he named, 'Sanderson his Hope of a North-west passage', now known as Sanderson's Hope off the west coast of Greenland; words that betray the jubilation he felt at seeing before him, as he mistakenly thought, the elusive North-west passage: 'No ice towards the north, but a great sea, free, large, very salt and blue, and of an unsearchable depth.' We would probably have reached 81° N. before encountering the Polar pack but we were not trying to establish a furthest north record for yachts and since there were no impediments in sight there was little merit to be acquired by going any further in that direction. We were bound round Vestspitzbergen and accordingly headed east.

Verlegenhuken at the entrance to Hinlopen Strait was sixty miles away almost due east. This is Fotherby's Point Desire which he named in 1614 and in normal years it marks the limit of open water along the north coast in the months from July to November. As long ago as 1924, in a book *With Seaplane and Sledge in the Arctic*, George Binney wrote: 'Of recent years the amelioration of ice conditions has been very marked; thirty years ago you could never be sure of rounding the northwest corner of Spitzbergen. Now you take for granted (after 1st July) open water as far as Verlegenhuken. It seems that the Atlantic current has become warmer and that its influence has extended north and east.'

The wind, which had been at north, now veered, forcing us off well south of east so that we fetched the coast at Mosselbukta, a bay ten miles south of Verlegenhuken. Either by being too far south or failing to keep a sharper look-out we missed sighting the curious island of Moffen which I much wanted to see. One would need good eyes anyway to spot it from a distance for it is only six feet high, sand and gravel, no vegetation at all. In the centre is a lagoon which, according to the *Pilot*, can be reached at high tide by small vessels. When Nordenskjold, the Swedish explorer who was the first to make the North-east passage, visited Moffen in 1861 he found the skeletons of thousands of walrus, killed by hunters. Mosselbukta, into which we penetrated before going about, is a spacious bay, originally known as Half-moon Bay and much favoured by whalers. Frederick Martens, mentioned before, reported that in mid-July (1671) there were many ships in the bay beset by ice. Nordenskjold, too, had to winter there in 1872 when ice prevented him from passing east of Verlegenhuken. Besides being the first to traverse the North-east passage, a feat he accomplished in two seasons 1878–9 in the 300-ton steam-sailing vessel *Vega*, Baron Nordenskjold, the eminent Swedish explorer, broke new ground in Vestspitzbergen and Northeastland and also in Greenland where he attempted the crossing of the ice-cap at its narrow southern end.

In the case of Spitzbergen there is good reason, I think, for what may appear to be over-much harping on early voyages and the names bestowed upon capes, bays, and islands by the hardy, enterprising whalers, the men who in fact did most of the exploring, as well as those given by their successors, the professional explorers. On nearly all coasts nowadays, even on some of the remotest, alterations have been made by man in the shape of bases or weather stations or there are enough hints of man's recent presence effectively to curtain off the distant past from the imagination of the present-day visitor. Not so on the north and east coasts of Vestspitzbergen. The odd cairn seen upon headland or island that alone betokens man's presence might have been built by the whalers themselves, just as the graves that one comes upon are occupied by those same men; and apart from these the coast looked as unknown, forlorn, and inhospitable as it had to them. Hence one could the more easily ignore the lapse of time, to regard Fotherby, Martens, and their like, as almost contemporaries, for one was seeing no more than they had seen; here, if anywhere, one of the aims and one of the rewards of the amateur sailor might be achieved, that which appealed to Belloc when he wrote:

In venturing in sail upon strange coasts we are seeking those first experiences, and trying to feel as felt the earlier man in a happier time, to see the world as they saw it.

Making long boards we were up near the head of Musselbukta before we could point north up the coast towards Verlegenhuken. Late on the afternoon of the 29th we weathered this noted cape and at once began meeting some scattered floes. They were nothing to worry about except that further down the Strait they looked a good deal less widely scattered than one might wish. By turning the cape we now had the bitterly cold north-east wind in our favour and we made haste to reach the shelter of Sorgfjord and the secure anchorage at Hecla Cove. Sorgfjord lies on the west side of the entrance to Hinlopen Strait and extends about five miles southwards. As we turned into Hecla cove late that evening the two small motor cruisers of our Cambridge friends were on the point of leaving, bound westwards. Shouts, a farewell wave, and the dipping of flags, and they were gone.

The bitter blast, which they would soon be facing, did not penetrate to Hecla cove. We could almost have dined on deck. Sparta, however, emphatically begins outside, so we went below for supper, a three-course banquet to celebrate our arrival at the entrance to Hinlopen Strait. And as we turned to go below I at any rate spared a thought for the Cambridge party, cold no doubt, and dining—if they had not already dined—upon Lifeboat biscuits and whatever the compiler of their twelve-man-day ration boxes might have ordained. The crowning mercy of our meal was the pudding, a pudding fit for a glass case, even though it were only a mock plum-pudding, its chief ingredient prunes, looking and tasting remarkably like the real thing, lubricated with rum butter, crowned with Hecla holly (a species unknown to Linnaeus), and carried in all alight and flaming by a triumphant Andrew.

The cove had evidently been the base of several bygone expeditions. Just above the little sandy beach were the remains of four huts, one of which, by sweeping out the snow, could easily have been made habitable. Another, circular in shape, had an eight foot high brick pillar in the middle, no doubt a base for some scientific instrument. Except for what had accumulated inside the hut and some drifts by the water's edge, the vicinity was entirely free from snow; and since the drifts, though exposed to the sun, showed no signs of melting it looks as if the winter snowfall must be removed by evaporation, or perhaps by wind as on the north side of Everest. There were four distinct beaches and most of the driftwood lay on the highest and therefore the oldest of them. On some islands south of Northeastland driftwood has been found at a height of 130 ft. above sea level, striking evidence according to the experts, not only of the land rising but of the slow rate of decomposition in these high latitudes, for several thousand years must have elapsed since the logs drifted ashore and the land began its slow rise.

On 30th July the wind had gone round to the south and blew so fresh that even in the cove we had difficulty in rowing against it. For Hinlopen Strait we needed a north wind or no wind at all, we therefore lay at earth. In Parry's day, if weather-bound in Hecla cove, one would have found abundant wild life to observe or more likely to shoot. Seventy reindeer and three bears were shot by his party, while of birds they noted ivory and glaucus gulls, terns, eider duck, grouse, and geese. Parry apparently intended using reindeer— presumably the tame variety—to haul his sledges on the North pole attempt, as Nordenskjold did successfully in 1872 when he crossed the Northeastland ice-cap. In the end Parry relied upon man-power for hauling two, large, flat-bottomed boats that could be fitted with either wheels or steel runners as the surface required. Travelling by night to take advantage of slightly colder conditions, and with the most severe labour, the party of twenty-two officers and bluejackets hauled these two heavy boats, *Enterprise* and *Endeavour*, for 200 miles as far as 82° 45′ N. or 435 miles short of the Pole. Many days elapsed before Parry discovered the heartbreaking truth that besides the terribly broken nature of the ice, they were also contending with a strong southerly drift, a drift so strong that if they rested for a day they lost almost as much as they had gained on the march of the previous day. So on 27th July 1827, when thirty-six days out, they turned back for Hecla cove and their ship H.M.S. *Hecla*, Parry admitting: 'I could not but consider it useless fatigue to officers and men and unnecessary wear and tear for the boats, to persevere any longer in the attempt.' Their record of furthest north stood for the next forty-eight years.

From the mouth of Sorgfjord the coast runs east for some three miles to C. Foster before turning south and opening up Hinlopen Strait. Thus the force of a wind blowing up the full fetch of the Strait is not felt until one is well clear of C. Foster. We learnt this next day when, deceived by the moderate wind inside C. Foster, we decided to make a start. Clear of the cape, and by then reefed down, we made a long board to the east across the strait, and having gone about found that on the return leg we could point no better than at the cape we had just left. In other words we were making no southing at all. So we started back for the cove. Within a mile of it, by the wind again falling light, we were led to think we had given up too easily and were merely chicken-hearted, but once more beyond Cape Foster we soon realised that conditions were no better. Prolonged beating in confined waters, where neither tack can be held for long and little ground is gained, is a wearing exercise; moreover the increasingly numerous floes driven up the Strait by the southerly wind meant that others besides the helmsman would have to be on deck for long spells. After a third futile attempt that evening the message sank home and we retired to Sorgfjord to await better times.

Even the ruins of four huts and raised beaches are not an inexhaustible sight. Besides Hecla cove there is an anchorage on the west side of the fjord off Graves Point, a name that aroused the morbid interest of the crew, their collection of bones far from complete. Thither we went and in the course of a peaceful night each of us in turn took a walk ashore, finding more raised beaches each with its load of driftwood, more derelict huts, and the graves. There were thirty of these, laid out in a line on the highest point, the heavy stones piled on each the only mark and memorial of some unnamed, forgotten man. The whalers penetrated as far east as this and the graves are most probably those of whaling men.

Early next morning a ship, the *Pole Star*, anchored half a mile south of us and after breakfast I rowed across for a gam with her captain. She might conceivably have come from south in which case they would know all about ice conditions in Hinlopen Strait. She was a vessel chartered by the Norwegian Polar Institute, a sealer type built for working among ice, carrying two helicopters and a bevy of bearded scientists. Having come by the north coast, as we had, they could tell us nothing about Hinlopen Strait, but unlike us they had sighted Moffen Is., landed on it by helicopter, and found there some forty walrus. So we had missed something worth seeing, the sea-horse in his native haunt. It is pleasant to think that they are returning to one of their old stamping grounds after having been persecuted almost to extinction.

A noted amateur in the walrus-killing line of business was Leigh Smith, the Victorian yachtsman already mentioned, whose yacht, by the way, like many others in those spacious days, was a vessel of 300 tons manned by a paid crew. Leigh Smith's two hobbies of shooting walrus and exploring were happily combined in several hazardous voyages to Spitzbergen, Northeastland, and as far east as Franz Josef Land, where in 1881 he lost his yacht *Eira* in the ice. A cape on Northeastland bears his name, a tribute to the man and to the sketch he made of that then almost unknown coast on a voyage in 1871. After the loss of *Eira*, crushed between pack-ice and shore-fast ice at C. Flora in Franz Josef Land, Leigh Smith's proceedings showed that he had the qualities needed in a successful seaman-explorer—leadership, resourcefulness, foresight, and the requisite know-how. The party of twenty-five officers and men wintered in an improvised hut and remained in good health in spite of having neither bedding nor fur clothing. Besides stores retrieved from *Eira* before she sank they killed and ate twenty-four walrus and thirty-four bears. The four ship's boats had been saved and during the winter they were made ready for the summer's voyage to Nova Zembla some 500 miles to the south. Sails were made and a quantity of fresh meat was boiled and tinned by the blacksmith. When they sailed on 21st June each boat had a compass, chronometer, sextant, charts. They were able to make a hot meal daily and brewed tea twice a day. On 1st August they landed at the western end of Matochkin Shar, the channel dividing Nova Zembla into two, and on the 3rd were picked up by Sir Allen Young in the relief ship *Hope*.

Another Victorian yachtsman with similar tastes though of less calibre as an explorer, was James Lamont. He made two voyages to Spitzbergen in 1858 and 1859, mainly in order to shoot as many seals and walrus as he possibly could, but he was also an enthusiastic amateur geologist. In spite of his ownership of a large yacht, yachting cannot be included among his hobbies; for in a book, *Seasons with the Seahorses*, published in 1861, he wrote: 'I sent the yacht round to Leith, while I travelled north by land, as I am not the least shamed to confess that I have a strong preference for land travelling, when it is practicable.'

But despite this professed dislike of the sea he knew what he was about and his remarks concerning ice navigation are worth quoting at length:

> I am perceived on this occasion (1858) that nothing could be more impracticable for ice navigation than a long fore-and-aft rigged schooner yacht, as in threading the intricate mazes of the ice there was no possibility of stopping her 'way' to avoid collisions, as is done by backing the topsails of a square-rigged vessel, and her frail planking and thin copper were exposed to constant destruction from the ice. Her dandified painted gigs were also totally unsuited for the rough work of pushing in amongst the ice in pursuit of seal and walrus; indeed it was very fortunate that we did not succeed in harpooning one of the latter mighty amphibiae from the yacht's boats, for my subsequent experience of the strength and ferocity of these animals leads me to believe that he would infallibly have pulled us all to the bottom of the sea.

Accordingly at Hammerfest Lamont chartered a boat such as the Norwegian sealers used, a thirty-ton sloop with a small square topsail, in which he cruised off the south coast of Edge Is. and in Storfjord, while his schooner yacht *Ginevra* spent the time out of harm's way in Isfjord. Incidentally he explored the head of Storfjord which is now called Ginevrabotnen, in which there is also a Lamont Is. On this second voyage he and his friend Lord Kennedy accounted for forty-six walrus, eighty-eight seal, eight polar bear, one white whale, and sixty-one reindeer, while another twenty walrus and forty seal were shot but sank. Not a bad bag. If the Victorians had an horror of slaughter they confined it to the slaughter of men, at least of white men, whereas now that animals are becoming scarce and men are proliferating we reserve most of our horror for the slaughter of the former. So much for our rude forefathers, but I confess that the sight of large quantities of game filled me with a similar blood-lust when I went in 1919 to what was then British East Africa, now Kenya. But it soon wore off and the time came when one would not so to speak cross the road for the sake of shooting an inoffensive buck however fine his head. The so-called dangerous game—elephant, rhino, buffalo, lion—were perhaps on a different footing, for the pursuit of these is less onesided and a slight mistake may lead to the demise of the hunter, or at least to his becoming the hunted instead of the hunter.

The skipper of *Pole Star* had no advice to offer concerning Hinlopen Strait, nor did he rate highly our chances of getting through. At this stage I rather agreed, especially after our experience of the previous day. Strong southerly winds might well be a local phenomenon like the northerlies that blow down the Portuguese coast in late summer. In 1954, inexperienced and ignorant of these northerlies, I was bringing *Mischief* home from the Mediterranean, and after beating against them for eighteen days, when somewhere off Oporto, our progress or lack of progress was brought to an end by a mutiny on the part of the crew. Hinlopen Strait itself is a good eighty miles in length, and beyond there is another hundred miles to get round Edge Is. In the southern half of the Strait there are many islands around which ice might accumulate; ice and islands together with head winds would pose some problems. However, as we were to learn later, the woes we fear do not come; worse ones do.

The following summary of attempts to pass through Hinlopen Strait, taken from the *Arctic Pilot*, might well omit some successful passages by small sealing vessels of which nothing would be heard:

> In 1827, during Parry's absence on his Polar journey, Lt. Foster surveyed the Strait as far south as the islets named after him, about forty miles within the northern entrance. He was able to identify almost every feature laid down on the old Dutch charts, thus showing it to have been delineated from observations made on the spot.
>
> In 1855 the map of Svalbard embodying the exploration of Duner and Nordenskjod (1861 and 1864) was published, carrying the survey to the southern end of the Strait. It was in 1864 that Nordenskjold rescued the crews of six boats that had been obliged to abandon their three walrus-hunting vessels beset in the ice south of Cape Leigh Smith and had succeeded in passing through the Strait from south to north.

In 1871 and twice in 1873 Leigh Smith attempted to pass through from north to south, but was stopped each time by ice; on the first and last occasion at the southern end of the Strait, and on the second attempt at the Foster Is.

In 1896 Sir Martin Conway succeeded in passing through from north to south but was held up by ice at its southern end and forced to return by the way he had come.

In 1900 De Geer, of the Swedish Arc of Meridian expedition, resurveyed the greater part of the Strait.

In August 1924 the Oxford University Expedition in the *Polarbjorn* and *Oiland* penetrated the Strait from north to south and ranged the southern coast of Northeastland, the return journey being made through the Strait.

In July 1925 Worsley in the *Island* passed through the Strait from north to south and succeeded in the circumnavigation of Northeastland.

In July 1930 the Norwegian vessel *Ringsael* passed through the Strait from north to south and proceeded along the southern coast of Northeastland without sighting any pack-ice.

Our fears about constant southerly winds were soon set at rest; we motored out that morning in fog and went on motoring throughout a completely windless day. As Dr. Johnson robustly remarks of those who indulge too much in hopes and fears: 'Let us cease to consider what may never happen, and what when it shall happen will laugh at human speculation.' Thanks to a timely lifting of the fog we were soon able to see where we were going and to choose the best line through the increasing floes. At its northern end the Strait is at its narrowest only some five miles wide and this tended to concentrate the floes. Twice we were brought to a stand and to some intricate manoeuvring in order to find a way through. In a vessel like *Baroque* with a large turning circle and at that time with no power in reverse, we needed to avoid getting into a cul de sac where the only remedy would have been to warp her out backwards. The question of darkness did not arise but I intended anchoring for the night in order to give the engine, or rather ourselves, some rest. As might be supposed of such unfrequented waters there are no recognised or recommended anchorages. We had to find our own and I thought that off the Foster Is. (a group of three small islets) would be the most likely bet. Solely owing to drifting ice, in most of the anchorages occupied in the course of the next few days I had reason to remember a remark made in one of the Mediterranean Pilot volumes about anchoring in some bight off the North African coast: 'Anchoring anywhere in this bight must be prompted by necessity and not by any hope of tranquillity.'

As we had hoped we found a place to anchor that evening off the easternmost of the Foster group. Foster, it will be remembered, was Parry's second-in-command. We were in seven fathoms, which was as close in as we dared go. There was a fine, big cairn on the summit of this 276 ft. high islet to which after supper Alan and I made a pilgrimage in order to leave in it a message for mankind. On our return I rashly agreed to Paul and Andrew taking a run ashore, for the wind had begun to pipe up from the north and they might have problems getting back. We missed their help, too, in a prolonged tussle with a large floe that had got athwart our cable. At midnight, when Paul and Andrew were on their way back in the dinghy, I turned in. But not for long. Stirred up by the ever-freshening northerly wind the ice was now on the move southwards and several large floes were already menacingly close. If we were not to be pushed on to the rocks it was high time to move. On the south side of the group the westernmost islet boasted the merest suspicion of a cove and we sounded our way in until we were within almost spitting distance of the shore without finding any bottom. Not far off I noticed a floe that was obviously aground so we crept close to that and let go the anchor in six fathoms. Andrew swung the lead like a professional. Admiration mingled with alarm as he swung that lethal weight in a complete circle, or several circles before letting it go. Some of my less efficient leadsmen of past voyages have contrived to land the lead on the foredeck instead of in the sea; fortunately they swung it only a modest half circle, for after a full-blooded swing such as Andrew used a misdirected lead might have gone through the deck. With the sea temperature 33° F. the taking of soundings, hauling in the wet line and coiling it for another cast, was not for boys. Sometimes it needed two, one to take over while the other got some feeling back into his hands. Why not an echo-sounder? I have thought about it but as Dr.

Johnson remarked: 'Conveniences are never missed where they were never enjoyed.'

We sailed after breakfast on a cold, dull morning, the air temperature 34° F. The wind remained fresh at north-west and when out of the lee of the Foster Is. we set all plain sail and bowled along at three or four knots, the ice-floes sparse and widely scattered. On the previous day we had made good nearly forty miles and our objective this day, Wilhelm Is., lay about the same distance further south and closer to the western side of the Strait which thereabouts is a good thirty miles wide. South of the Foster group there is a long string of islets, the Vaigat Is., which encumber the middle of the Strait for a distance of fifteen miles. Most of them are named after members of Nordenskjold's and other Swedish expeditions. Between the Vaigat islands and the coast of Northeastland there is a five-mile wide channel and even there the floes were far enough apart for us to sail unhindered. With a leading wind such as we now enjoyed one can weave a way through moderately close floes, whereas with a head wind one would be either running the boat off or getting her in irons. This north wind was a blessing, too, in that it stopped any more ice coming up from the south where it appeared to be pretty thick. At midday *Pole Star* passed bound south and in the afternoon we could still see her mast sticking up above the ice far to the south-east. Judging by her frequent changes of direction she seemed to be working through heavy ice.

By evening we were east of the Von Otter Is., the southernmost of the Vaigat group, with Wilhelm Is. still ten miles away and a lot of ice in between. Forgetting Wilhelm Is. for the moment we turned west and at 8 p.m. anchored off the south-west corner of Von Otter Is. where low, gently shelving gravel slopes enclosed a bay of moderate depths, free from floes. To our eyes, attuned to a harsh landscape of rock and ice, with only logs of driftwood to remind us of the existence of trees, Von Otter Is. looked friendly, almost benign. Having had our *pasta sciuta*, followed by a prime duff of noble proportions, we were relaxing on deck, taking the air, admiring the placid but austere scene, when a Polar bear strolled down to the beach. One had the impression that he felt satisfied, that he felt as we did: 'Fate cannot harm me, I have dined today.' Taking no notice of *Baroque* he launched himself off and swam in leisurely fashion past the boat barely thirty

Baroque anchored off Wilhelm Is.

yards away. Bears, I believe, are now protected in Svalbard, and none too soon for there cannot be many left. In many voyages north I had never seen a Polar bear and this alone made our Spitzbergen voyage worth while. During his anchor watch later that night Alan saw a female with two cubs.

I set great store on our making Wilhelm Is. It is a big island and its southern shore, where I wanted to be, still lay twenty miles away. As well as big, it is 1820 ft. high and from somewhere on its southern slopes I counted on seeing far to the south, far enough, I hoped, to be able to weigh up our chances of getting through. Pole Star had evidently met a lot of ice, and though she was well to the east of our course, possibly bound round Nordaustland, I did not feel over sanguine about our own prospects. When we sailed on 3rd August the wind was still fresh at north, so fresh that we rolled in a reef. It was not until we drew near Thumb Point, the easternmost point of Wilhelm Is., that we met much ice. There we dropped the mains'l and proceeded under stays'l alone. From a couple of miles south of the island another string of islets stretches southwards for ten miles and in the gap between Wilhelm Is. and the northernmost of this string the ice at first sight looked impenetrable. I had begun to fear that this would beat us when Paul from the crosstrees reported open water beyond this barrier and also a possible lead through it. Once more one learnt not to judge ice conditions without a close inspection or without the use of the highest possible view point. We got through with little trouble, reset the mains'l, and ran on towards the island. We were still a good mile off shore when, not liking the colour of the water, I thought it time to take some soundings. None too soon either, for we were in two fathoms of water and sailing fast towards the shore. Turning away we downed the mains'l and anchor in three fathoms, still a mighty long way from the beach.

For the last two days of overcast skies and northerly winds the air temperature had seldom risen above 35° F. Considering the amount of ice about that was reasonable enough and we had nothing to complain about. At sea between 79° and 80° N., even in August, one could hardly expect to feel warm. 'Comfort must not be expected by folks that go a-pleasuring,' as Byron says. That evening, with a rising glass, the sky cleared, the sun came out, and the brown, barren slopes of Wilhelm Is. assumed a warm, welcoming glow. After tea I rowed ashore alone, for

in view of the long row the less weight in the dinghy the better. Some
snow drifts some 500 ft. above the sea were the chosen vantage point
towards which I plodded slowly up a boulder-strewn gully, resolved
not to turn round for a glance southwards until I had reached them.
I was well rewarded. On that clear, calm, sunny evening I reckoned
I could see forty miles or more, at least as far as Edge Is., and all the
way was a broad lead of open water bounded on the west by the coast
of Barents Is., and on the east by a field of unbroken ice. Aware of
how quickly ice conditions can change I had an uneasy feeling that
we ought to push on that night; but there are never any lack of reasons for doing nothing—if you practise inaction, as the Taoist doctrine
preaches, nothing is left undone—and mindful of how little rest we had
had in the last few days I decided to stay. Back at the boat they told me
another bear had been seen and were surprised, perhaps disappointed,
that we had not met.

For all the rest we got that night we might as well have gone on.
Twice we had to shift our berth on account of ice drifting athwart the
cable, threatening to uproot the anchor or to damage the bowsprit.
Before breakfast I went up the hill again, satisfied myself that conditions were unchanged, and after breakfast we started off in a flat
calm—ideal conditions for motoring. For most of the morning we had
on our port hand the long chain of islets, some almost hidden by the
floes that had banked up around them. Messrs. Lamont and Leigh
Smith would have had a field day, for on the floes there were many
seals. By noon we had C. Payer abeam, or rather the place where the
cape had been. A glacier has overflowed the cape and now projects
into the sea well beyond it. This cape marks the easternmost point
of Vestspitzbergen and the entrance on that side to Hinlopen Strait,
while on the Northeastland side the entrance point is an indeterminate
glacier tongue. We were therefore through the Strait but still had to
pass the east coasts of Barents Is. and Edge Is., a distance of about
sixty miles.

A few miles south of the ice-engulfed C. Payer is Heley Sound, a
narrow channel between Vestspitzbergen and Barents Is., leading into
Ginevrabotnen, the head of Storfjord explored by Lamont. It was
named after William Heley, an English supercargo in the whaling fleet
in 1617, but it was not until 1858 that Johannes Nielsen of Tromso sailed

Building a cairn on Barents Is.,
looking towards the western end of Freemansund

through it and proved it to be a strait. Before then all charts showed it
as a creek running northwards from Ginevrabotnen. Heley Sound was
therefore a possible escape route for us had we felt desperate enough
to take it. The *Pilot* has this to say:

> In 1869 Heleysundet was explored by Lamont who called it Hell
> Sound and recorded as follows: 'The sound itself appeared like a
> winding river, being not more than four or five hundred yards across
> and two miles long. High precipices bounded the north side...
> Between these contracted shores a tremendous tide was running out
> at some 8 knots, carrying with it quantities of ice. On the opposite
> side an enormous glacier projected from Barents Is. far out into the
> East sea.' Two days after making these observations Lamont passed
> through in a boat at the top of flood tide, which sets north-eastward,
> and returned with the ebb. In August 1897 Arnold Pike, finding large
> floes in Freemansundet, steamed through Heleysundet in *Victoria*.
> He reported the navigation was most difficult on account of the vio-
> lent currents, the rate of which he estimated at 10 knots.

For the last few days I had been pondering the question of whether to
complete our circumnavigation of Vestspitzbergen by way of Freemansund between Barents Is. and Edge Is. or to go outside Edge Is. direct
into the Barents Sea. The latter course would make a more complete
and satisfying job of it and if we should meet a lot of ice off Edge Is.
there would still be Freemansund to fall back on. In view of the mass
of ice close to the eastward I thought we might well be stopped on
the way round Edge Is.; on the other hand I was not all that keen on
Freemansund which likewise has strong currents though nothing like
so fierce as those of Heley Sound. Besides that there might be a concentration of ice in this comparatively narrow channel which averages
three to four miles in width. That evening when we were some ten miles
east of the Freemansund entrance we did in fact meet a concentration
of floes, and having got through them I decided to stand on to the
south in order to go round Edge Is. When a nice breeze set in from the
east we stopped the engine and set all plain sail, and at 10 p.m. on a
lovely, sunny evening, with the way ahead still clear as far as one could
see, I turned in feeling almost confident that we should get through.

At midnight Andrew reported ice ahead and on climbing to the cross-trees I saw what looked like a solid wall of ice stretching out from the coast of Edge Is. to merge with the field of ice that all day had lain along our port hand. We were still two or three miles short of this seeming barrier and in any other circumstances I should have closed with it for a proper look, to see how close the floes really lay and whether there was open water in sight beyond them. But the probably easier and certainly shorter alternative of Freemansund was too tempting and unluckily I decided to take it, thus setting the scene for another regrettable incident. Putting about we ran off to the north-west and were soon back off C. Heuglin, the northernmost point of Edge Is. and ten miles from the entrance to Freemansund.

CHAPTER VI

FREEMANSUND AND HOMEWARDS

There is nothing so distressing as running ashore—unless there is also a doubt as to which continent the shore belongs.

LECKY'S WRINKLES.

FREEMANSUND is thus described in the *Pilot*:

> Freemansundet, a strait about 22 miles in length, with a least width of about 2½ miles, separates Edgeoya from Barentsoya, and was named after Alderman Freeman, a director of the Muscovy Company, who visited Svalbard in 1619. The strait is reported to be too shallow and rocky to admit the passage of any but small craft, and Nordenskjold, when looking down on it from an elevation of 1066 ft. at the summit of Kapp Lee, the southern entrance point at the western end of the strait, observed that it appeared to be much encumbered with sand-banks. However, Captain E. Lund of Hammerfest sailed through the strait in August 1847 and in August 1870 Von Heuglin passed through along the southern side of the strait. Freemansundet is entered from eastwards between Kapp Heuglin (78°15′ N. 22°56′ E.) and Kapp Waldburg, the south-eastern extremity of Barentsoya, about 9 miles westward. Foul ground extends about 15 miles northward and north-westward of Kapp Heuglin and it is reported that Kapp Waldburg is foul also. Zeiloyane are two islets lying in the middle of the eastern entrance, about 4 miles west-north-westward of Kapp Heuglin.

The remark about the strait being too shallow and rocky for the passage of any but small craft is out of date; both the Admiralty chart and the Norwegian chart show a line of soundings which give a least depth of six fathoms near the eastern entrance increasing to twenty-four fathoms at the western end. However, these two charts did not agree about the Zeiloyane islets, either as to their position or number.

The breeze having died we were again under engine when at 4 a.m. I took over the watch from Alan. What followed is not easy to explain and still less easy to excuse. Perhaps, having spent the last three days mostly on deck and enjoyed only disturbed nights, I was not as bright as I should have been. Zeiloyane, the two islets mentioned above, were in sight ahead and with the west-going ebb under us we were rapidly approaching them. We had already discovered that west of C. Heuglin along the north coast of Edge Is. the water was shoal and we intended passing north of the Zeiloyane islets. I had my eyes fixed on one but the northernmost looked to me like a spit of land projecting from the coast of Barents Is. What with the engine and the tide which, as we neared the islets seemed to gather speed for its rush through the channel, we must have been making seven or eight knots over the ground. Before I had really hoisted in what was happening we were heading between the two islets which are a mile or so apart. To attempt to pass between unknown islets however wide apart they may be is always a hazardous proceeding. A shoal extended the whole way between the two and the rate we were going ensured our being carried right up on the back of it before we ground to a stop.

If the crew thought the old man had taken leave of his senses, as they must have done, they studiously refrained from comment. As soon as the tide slackened a bit we ran out a kedge astern bringing the warp forward to the winch. The engine, as we knew, had no power in reverse and the winch alone failed to budge her. Circumstances had combined to make things as difficult as they could be. Although the ebb had been running for an hour or more we must have gone on at or near the highest level of water; it was three days after full moon so that the tides were taking off. The differences between high and low water proved to be only around two feet, which in one way was a good thing because the boat remained more or less upright. What happens, I think, is that when the ebb starts running west the water piles up in the narrow, twenty-two-mile-long strait and thus continues to rise or at any rate maintains its level at the eastern end when it should be falling. Something similar occurs at the eastern end of the Magellan Straits where the water is pent up in the First and Second Narrows with the result that the west-going and east-going streams continue running in the channel for three hours after high and low water by the shore.

There, too, as we found in Freemansund, the duration of slack water is barely noticeable.

Our next move was to take out half the ballast and jettison it over the side. We had no choice. The nearest islet was half-a-mile away and in the absence of any appreciable slack water there was no question of rowing a heavily-laden dinghy that far. In spite of a strong westerly wind blowing out of the strait—a wind that blew incessantly for the next few days—the sea remained calm and the boat motionless. There was thus no fear of the boat damaging herself by pounding, but we had something else to worry about. When the west-going stream started again it brought with it numerous ice-floes, large and small. The big ones grounded on the edge of the shoal about fifty yards away where they furnished a kind of protective barrier. There were, however, gaps in the barrier through which any piece of ice that drew less than six or seven feet of water found its way, and by driving past the boat at a rate of several knots threatened disaster to either our rudder or our propeller. Bits of ice moving at that rate, even if they weighed only half a ton or so, could neither be stopped nor diverted with boat-hooks. Watching a small floe apparently on a collision course we could only hold our breath and hope. Twice the rudder sustained a savage blow. Nor were we much better off when the tide turned, when those that had already passed came back with the flood.

No one doubted that we should get her off in time—at least no doubts were expressed—but I felt that we had only to stay there long enough for the worst to happen. Damage to the rudder would be bad enough but if the propeller were damaged the chances of getting off would be much reduced; for by now it was clear that we must get her facing the way she had come so that the engine could be used to advantage. We were a sitting target for these floes, dependent entirely upon luck. We could not afford to be aground three days as *Mischief* had been on her first voyage in '54 when she stuck on a reef in a Patagonia fjord. In the course of three days three tons of ballast were ferried ashore and she floated off. In the meantime drifting ice of far smaller dimensions than the Freemansund floes stripped the propeller blades and bent the shaft. Happily on that occasion, by being away on the ice-cap at the time, I was not only free from blame but also escaped the strains and stresses resulting from the stranding of a vessel, especially for the owner.

In the afternoon, near high water, we made several attempts to pull her head round, for until we could get her pointing the way she had come and so make full use of the engine we should never get off. Having got us into this mess I at least should have had skilly for supper, instead we finished up with one of David's increasingly majestic duffs. Care weighing heavy upon me, I could only toy with this, notwithstanding the advice of that strong-minded gastronome Dr. Oppimian—'Whatever happens in this world, never let it spoil your dinner.' No doubt the reverend doctor had never assisted at a stranding, a stranding that might well become a shipwreck if a piece of ice with *Baroque*'s name on it hit her in a vital spot. The crew having disposed of the duff we turned with renewed vigour to taking out the remainder of the ballast and emptying all the water tanks but for a few gallons for immediate use. The crew worked like heroes, Paul groping away in the bilge prizing out the slimy chunks of pig-iron—some weighing eighty to ninety pounds—from the filthy bed where for years they had lain undisturbed. In no time all were once more coated from head to foot in black, oily sludge. Besides all the ballast and most of the water, we threw overboard an old flax mainsail that we had been carrying as a spare. It dated from the days of *Mischief* and when wet, as the sails stowed on a rack in the peak always were, it must have weighed about four hundredweight. Normally I get a lot of harmless pleasure from throwing overboard superfluous gear. The mainsail might be included in that category, but certainly not the ballast.

We had already lost a kedge and now Andrew went off in the dinghy with the big Fisherman type anchor hanging over the stern ready to drop in the selected spot. This anchor weighed about a hundredweight and we were reconciled to losing that, too, for if she came off we were not going to risk going aground again while making an effort to retrieve it. The boat was now a lot lighter and in the course of the night by heaving away on the firmly embedded big anchor, little by little we brought her head round until at last she pointed in the right direction. The westerly wind still blew vigorously out of the strait. It seemed to be an almost permanent local feature and later when we were trying to make headway through the strait we had good reason to curse it. As they say in Africa, cross the river before you start reviling the crococile's mother, and at this juncture, twenty-four hours after the first stranding, we wanted a west wind, the more the better. So with the whole mainsail and staysail set and drawing, the flood tide making, the engine flat out, the kedge warp quivering under the strain of the winch, and a subdued cheer from the crew, she began to move.

The big anchor had played its part, and having got in all the warp we could before it grew wide on the beam we cut it, and a moment later came to a shuddering stop alongside a large floe grounded on the edge of the shoal. We lost no time in playing our last card, another small kedge anchor of only about twenty-five pounds' weight. Surprisingly enough this diminutive anchor took good hold, and as we winched in on it—the sails, the engine, and the tide all working hard to assist—the boat reluctantly bumped her way off. We were too anxious to be clear of this baleful shoal to bother with the little anchor. This, too, became a sacrifice together with two other anchors, all the ballast, and the old mainsail. Our only remaining anchor was the sixty-pound CQR which we normally used.

Giving the northernmost Zeiloyane islet the widest possible berth we headed for Freemansund, the ebb tide by then having begun to run. But even with the tide under us we made little progress against the westerly wind, so we sheered off to the north to anchor off the southeast corner of Barents Is. where we obtained a bit of a lee. In this short sail, while the absence of any ballast did not seem to make the boat unduly tender, the complaints that came from the rudder could hardly be ignored. After the two blows it had sustained from the ice, the fact that it was still there and still steering the ship was more surprising than the play one felt in the tiller and the occasional groans from under the counter.

When we sailed out next morning and were clear of the shelter of Barents Is. we faced the same west wind. Nevertheless we managed to make good some five miles inside the strait before the turn of the tide obliged us to make for the north shore where behind a little cape we found less wind and less current. Half a mile to the east the high ice front of the Freeman glacier projected well into the water. From this floes frequently broke off though few of them found their way into our shallow bay. Before beginning the long haul homewards we needed ballast and water and I had intended to look for these at some anchorage in Storfjord where one might expect to be free from the strong winds and currents of Freemansund. On going ashore that evening, however, I found a small trickle of water that if dammed up we could collect, as well as an assortment of reasonably sized stones. Like the plums in a poor man's duff they were not that plentiful and would need gathering, but we might go further and fare worse so I decided to stock up here. The plain that extended inland looked as barren as the beach, yet on it I counted eighteen reindeer busily grazing. Like yaks, they seem to subsist or even thrive on a diet of gravel slightly flavoured with moss.

The evil day had at last come when, our bread finished, we had to go on to biscuit, and since the supply of that was not abundant we agreed on a remarkably small daily ration. After a large dose of stiff porridge most of us went without the breakfast allotment, saving it for lunch when it could be used to convey to the mouth cheese, sardine or peanut butter, all more interesting than marmalade. We were lying a good 400 yards out and when deciding to fill up here with ballast and water I had assumed we could bring the boat much closer to the beach. Andrew went off in the dinghy to take soundings and when he found the water started to shoal almost under the bows I regretted my decision and had half a mind to push on. However, we blew up the inflatable dinghy and set to work with that and the pram dinghy, our working hours being limited by the duration of the ebb tide. The west wind, we found, almost sufficed to offset the effect of the west-going stream. When the flood ran, with the wind behind it, work had to stop.

Since the amount of stone that could be got into the space occupied by the jettisoned pig-iron, which we estimated to be nearly three tons, would not weigh nearly so much, we made additional space for ballast by emptying the food lockers under the bunks on either side of the cabin, stowing more in the main food locker forward which by now was half empty. Even when stones had been shoved into every available hole and corner the pessimists reckoned that we should not be carrying more than two tons. Others put it as high as two and a half tons, while Andrew, despising guesswork, invoked the aid of Archimedes and his well-known Principles. Weighing on our spring balance a piece of iron and a piece of stone, he then measured the volume of water that each displaced and in due course, all calculations made and checked, announced smugly that our stone ballast would weigh exactly a quarter of the original pig-iron, or rather less than a ton. So much for what Goethe called the charnel house of science. Nothing has an uglier look than reason when it is not on our side and we hastened to tell Andrew what he could do with Archimedes and his bath-water.

For most of next day the wind proved too strong for the tide and it was not until after supper that ferrying began again. By midnight, when only one load of stones and two of water were needed to complete the job, a brief puff of wind discouraged the crew. I was set on getting away on the morning tide and the crew, seeing my disappointment, fell to again. By 2 a.m. we were getting the dinghies on board for the last time. Ever since the stranding they had cheerfully given all they had in back-breaking, wet, and grimy toil to retrieve a bad situation. Accordingly, on the morning of 10th August, the west wind much less than usual, we completed the passage of Freemansund, homeward bound at last. As we had suspected, the west wind prevailed only in Freemansund. For the rest of the day we drifted and sailed fitfully across a windless Storfjord. All that night we were puzzled and disquieted by a distant sound, a sort of 'melancholy, long, withdrawing roar', that might have been the growl of pack-ice or of waves breaking on a shingle beach, except that we had seen no ice in Storfjord, nor in our tour round Spitzbergen had we come across any beaches of shingle. In thick weather and light airs we made our way slowly down the west coast of Storfjord, seeing little except for an occasional glimpse of a glacier whose brightness even the fog could not hide. Of these there are no less than ten on this seventy-mile stretch of coast.

The coast runs almost due south to Sorkapp which we passed when north-bound on 4th July in brilliant sunshine. It would have been a useful point from which to take our departure but this time fog hid everything. On a long voyage taking one's departure is a navigational luxury rather than a necessity and, according to Scoresby, whalers homeward bound from the Greenland Sea had only the vaguest notion of where they were starting from. As he writes:

When a ship has on board an ample cargo course is directed immediately homeward. It is not unusual for a ship to bear away without the navigators having first obtained any certain knowledge as to their longitude, not having perhaps seen any land for some weeks or even months; having neither a chronometer on board, nor the means of taking a lunar observation; they set out ignorant of the meridian on which they sail and sensible to their being liable to an error of five or six degrees of longitude. In such cases they steer a south-westerly course by the compass. If they steer too far to the eastward they make the coast of Norway, and if too far to the westward they probably make the Faeroes.

In other words, you can't go wrong. It all sounds like the rough and ready sailing directions for a Nova Scotiaman bound for Barbadoes: 'Steer south until the butter melts and then turn east.' Although we started off on a rather better footing than the homeward bound whalers we, too, were not fussy about our next landfall; except that Norway had to be avoided, indeed the whole of the North Sea, for we wished to return west-about. We would therefore take the wind as it served and if we got pushed too far to the west would call at the Faeroes for bread and water, otherwise we would make for Lerwick in the Shetlands. Having been there before I had a slight preference for the Faeroes, but as it happened we made neither.

For the first few days in the open sea the state of the rudder gave us more concern than any possible shortage of ballast which, if Andrew and Archimedes were right, might result in a capsize. The boat appeared to be no more tender than before and we never thought of reducing sail on that account, but the groans emanating from the rudder and the increasing play that could be felt were constant and unpleasant reminders of the possibility of losing it. To avoid imposing on it any additional strain we determined not to heave-to; instead, if the occasion arose, we lay-a-try with the helm unlashed. Meantime, during one's spell at the tiller, when the horrid spectre really took shape, one could pass the time devising ways of coping if the rudder did at last come adrift. What would Hornblower have done, I asked myself, and curiously enough we found the answer to that in a copy of *The Commodore* which happened to be on board. From either quarter stream a half-filled barrel (or presumably any suitable weight) and by heaving in the port warp and letting out the starboard, or vice versa, steer accordingly, learning as you go by trial and error. Nothing could be simpler.

Until we reached home waters we made slow work of it, seldom
having a favourable slant of wind. The further south we got the more
contrary the weather, and in consequence the more occupation we had
in the way of pumping as well as the stitching of sails. The mainsail, a
good, strong terylene sail, had been put together on the wrong prin-
ciple. The cloths, instead of running up and down, ran fore and aft,
so that if a seam opened near the leach it might, and often did, open
half-way across the sail towards the luff. Moreover the seams had been
machine stitched with thread that one would hardly trust for a trouser-
button. If the jib or stays'l needed repair they could be taken below
whereas the mains'l had to be attended to on deck as and when the
weather permitted. Nearly a fortnight after leaving Spitzbergen, and
two months since we had first crossed it, we recrossed the Arctic Circle,
an occasion that had to be suitably marked. Its a poor heart that never
rejoices and at sea the galley, or what comes out of it, is probably the
most likely cause of rejoicing. In preparation for this banquet more
or less all hands mustered in the galley, each bent on showing what
he could do; nor was there any fear of too many cooks spoiling the
broth because each was too intent on his own masterpiece to meddle
with that of anyone else. Alan, sole architect and creator, led off with
the *hors d'oeuvre*—sardines submerged in a pungent mixture of tomato
puree and curry powder, tastefully draped with melted cheese; Paul,
possibly with left-wing tendencies, gave birth to Borscht, thick as glue
and withal luscious; after these lofty flights David brought us back to
earth with homely Cottage Pie, while Andrew, a dab hand at pastry,
clinched matters with an outsize apple tart. Cocoa laced with rum followed as a corrective.

Three southerly gales in a row drove us so far to the west that Thor-
shavn, in the Faeroes, became the likeliest target. We had no charts
for the Faeroes and on 1st Sept. when we were only a few miles off
the weather was so thick that I preferred not to try to find the place.
Instead of waiting for the fog to clear, the wind still fair for Scotland,
we decided to carry on for Stornoway. At this time the weather round
the British Isles was extremely unsettled with gale warnings in force
for most areas. A low in the Irish Sea was said to be moving north
bringing with it a force ten gale. On the night of 3rd Sept. we sighted
the C. Wrath light, our first landfall, and although the night was dirty

enough the wind was nothing like force ten. Being too far east we failed to weather C. Wrath and in consequence spent a day bucketing about in a confused sea and not enough wind with the islands of Rona and Sula Sgeir in sight to the north. At least Paul and Alan had the pleasure of seeing again the islands that had been their objective on their first cruise. By the evening we were inside Lewis in calm waters, the wind so slight that we turned on the engine. Whereupon a gush of oil and water mixed obliged Paul quickly to turn it off, for obviously a liner had cracked or had a hole in it. The engine had evidently been living on borrowed time and we had reason to be thankful that this had not happened when we were aground or coming through Freemansund.

On the night of 6th Sept. we sailed cautiously into Stornoway to anchor until morning when we went alongside to take on water and bread. As usual David disappeared for the day. So far as I know he had not a penny but he was no doubt rich in tall Spitzbergen yarns, rich enough to induce someone to pay for his drinks. I came across him on the quay some time after midnight pretending he was a Polar bear. Persistent head winds made for a slow passage through the Minches and then a hard south-easterly gale drove us well to the west of Tory Island off the north-west corner of Ireland. The prospect of having to sail down the west coast and of having no doubt to make frequent tacks to keep clear of the land was far from pleasing; but before we were quite reconciled to it the wind veered to south-west and soon rose to gale force. Whereupon we ran off to the east to enjoy a wonderful day's sailing with the rugged north coast of Ireland close aboard. Later in the day, in order to have a fair tide in Rathlin Sound, we slowed her down by dropping the mains'l and even so she continued to run at close on four knots. We surged through Inishtrahull Sound just as the lighthouse lit up and by daybreak we were through the North Channel and off the Maidens by breakfast time. This was the first really fair wind we had had since leaving Spitzbergen and two days later another favourable gale gave us a final shove home. Having rounded Lands End at midnight of the 19th we anchored off Lymington river at midnight of the 21st. In the course of this fast run up Channel we were twice nearly run down by small coasters, having on both occasions to gybe hurriedly to avoid a collision. On a rough night in a lively sea a yacht's oil lamps might not easily be seen, and in the intoxication of *Baroque's* wild rush for home we had forgotten to hoist the radar reflector. But close quarter situations with steamers, either large or small, should be avoided however many lights or radar reflectors one may be showing.

Since the engine had evidently had it we could hardly make bad worse by using it, so on the next day, a Sunday, we motored up the river. Through impatience and the desire to have done we started too soon on the young flood and owing to lack of water and the week-end traffic we twice took the mud. The first time must have been in sight of the Royal Lymington Clubhouse, yet notwithstanding this unseaman-like approach, as we passed, they gave us their customary finishing gun. For me it was not a happy return: a friend boarded us in the river to tell me that my sister with whom I lived, and with whom I had spoken by telephone from Stornoway, had died suddenly on the day we left there. But it had been a happy voyage as well as a notable voyage in that we had accomplished our aim. On recent voyages this has not often hap-pened; but, as I have said before somewhere, there is little point in setting out for a place that one is almost certain to reach. Of course, if failures become too frequent there may be something wrong with the objective, too ambitious perhaps, or even something wrong with one-self, too fainthearted; yet if the blame for failure can be placed fairly and squarely upon natural causes, such as ice, it need not be taken too much to heart. I have in mind Scoresby Sound which we made three attempts to reach. Two of them were certainly frustrated by ice, while on the third the crew were unwilling to press on. Big mountains are seldom climbed at the first attempt which is more often a pioneering effort, breaking the trail for those who follow. Whether successful or not, on these voyages of mine there is a little of the pioneer's reward as well as four months' sailing to look back on with pleasure, four months of endeavour to mull over, and that much more experience to store away. Experience is said to be the name men give to their mistakes and of the experience I gained in Spitzbergen that may well be true. Much, if not all, depends on the crew. I had with me a good crew and if a man chooses to put his ship aground in Freemansund that is what he needs.

PART TWO

West Greenland

1975

CHAPTER VII

FINDING A CREW

B Y THE AUTUMN OF 1974 circumstances had changed for the worse. I had now to face living entirely alone like a Himalayan ascetic in his mountain cave—a spacious cave, I admit, far too spacious for one man. Instead of making it easier, this made it harder to get away either for long or short periods, what with the dogs who shared master's cave and other considerations. Increasing feebleness would oblige me to swallow the anchor some day and that day was not far off. Dwindling resources, too, along with inflated bills plus 25% VAT. Like Tallulah Bankead, in similar hard times, one began to wonder where the next magnum was coming from. In this weak frame of mind I even questioned the making of another voyage, to regard *Baroque*'s circumnavigation of Spitzbergen as a fitting occasion, a memorable last act, upon which to ring down the curtain. Wisdom certainly pointed that way but whenever there has been a choice between wisdom and what many might regard as folly I have usually chosen the latter. Strenuousness, we are told, is the immortal path, sloth is the way of death. Well aware of this truth I left the question for the moment, with a slight bias in favour of action.

My real hope was that in the course of the winter, as has usually happened in the past, someone who had a mind to take part would write to ask if I had any plans for the coming year. This would act as a spur and be also a commitment, for to assure oneself that a voyage will be undertaken is not as binding as a promise to take someone else. Meantime I made infrequent journeys to Lymington to commune with *Baroque* and bit by bit to bring back for overhaul all the running rigging—the wire for renewal where needed, ropes to be turned end for end, and all the blocks, some twenty-five or so, to be taken apart, greased, and varnished. Wooden blocks ought to be cherished for even now they are not easily found. Soon the only place to buy them—at antique prices—will be those antique shops with a marine flavour, along with ship's wheels, copper navigation lamps, and gimballed brass cabin lamps. Several years ago a Southampton ship's chandler confessed to me that he had sold his entire stock of beautiful wooden blocks with bronze sheaves and pins to a scrap-metal merchant who had promptly burnt the lot to retrieve the metal.

Without any ballast at all *Baroque* rode high in the water. The Spitzbergen rock she had brought home had been taken out and dumped on the quay and I had not yet acquired the necessary three tons of pig-iron. The pile of stones on the quay had steadily diminished; rock gardeners, amateur geologists, and souvenir hunters had been chiselling away at it until little remained. The Lymington Town Sailing Club took the biggest bit they could find and having affixed a suitably inscribed brass plate presented it to me at one of their meetings. Weighing some thirty pounds it is on the heavy side for a paper weight but it makes an admirable door-stop.

The rudder which had sustained severe blows from passing floes when she was aground had been repaired. A new heel fitting was required and that the rudder had remained in place until we got home was a source of wonder. The engine had been taken out, a feat of some ingenuity if the amount of wrecking done was to be kept within bounds. By means of two small holes bored in the roof of the doghouse a chain lift could be inserted to raise the monster from its bed and then with not more than an inch to spare manoeuvred through the door opening on to the cockpit.

Either out of friendly curiosity or puzzled, perhaps, by some of the oddities that from time to time figure amongst my crews, many people ask how they are obtained. Do I resort to crimps or press-gangs? The method or lack of method employed in 1975 is a sample, though since this proved to be one of the more difficult years it is not quite a fair one. Contrary to my hopes the gloom of the winter months was not relieved by enquiries from anyone interested in making a northern voyage. Such enquiries are valuable because they show that the enquirer is keen, and it is better to be approached than to have to approach someone, someone who may get it into his head, perhaps rightly, that he is doing you a favour by coming. And, as I have said, that winter I particularly needed some encouragement, better still a commitment, to making a voyage. But no would-be voyagers, either youthful or elderly, showed any interest in *Baroque* or any plans I might have for using her in the summer. So when March came I was a worried man, for instead of taking this lack of interest as the required signal to stay quietly at home it made me the more obstinately determined to find a crew and go somewhere. The aforesaid crimps, had they been still in business, would have been of no use. The ships they catered for were on the point of sailing and the essence of the contract was that the crew they provided should not wake up or recover from a drunken stupor until the ship was safely at sea, whereas I needed my crew at least a fortnight before sailing to help in fitting-out. Numerous feelers were put out to the proliferating Sailing Schools, Adventure Centres, and such like, but none of them touched anything. My first victim, a young man whose home was not far from Barmouth, came by chance, some friends having put me in touch with him. Nicholas was a rolling stone who so far had gathered no moss, nor any polish either. Among the many other jobs that he had held for a time was that of an instructor at an Adventure Centre in Scotland so that he had sailed a boat. He was currently driving a van in Swansea. First impressions were favourable and delight at having at last made a start inclined one to take a good deal for granted. Looking a bit like a bird himself, red-headed at that, bird-watching proved to be his real forte. Meantime the fact that he was employed driving a van ear-marked him for looking after *Baroque*'s engine.

In spite of our long partnership in Africa and the Himalayas in the 'thirties Eric Shipton and I seldom correspond and in fact seldom know at any given moment where the other is. A letter from him therefore came as a surprise, a welcome surprise because it asked me to consider taking with me his youngest boy John. When they bring you a heifer be ready with the rope, and anyway, for old time's sake this was a request that could hardly be refused. Assuming he would be a likely lad I took him on unseen. We talked by telephone but did not meet until later on at Lymington. Young John had spent the last three years bumming his way round the world and in the course of this had crewed on passage-making yachts. He therefore had ocean-going experience though some of the questions he asked and things he did during our first days at sea gave me some concern for those same yachts. However, he soon became a competent hand, uncomplaining, indefatigably

cheerful, and ready to turn his hand to anything. I say uncomplain-
ingly because although he had the wettest berth, forward of the galley
and too near the forward hatchway, so that its occupant has to live
under a permanent polythene canopy, John took this in his stride. Like
father, he loved talking and arguments, but had such volubility, such a
rush of words to the mouth, that when I was concerned I had to have
everything repeated in slow time before I got the message.

The manager of the yard where *Baroque* lives put me in touch with
Andrew Horsfield, a student at London University who had had some
ocean-going experience. From what I was told I felt he would be my
key-man, less volatile than the other two, and indeed he proved a tower
of strength, reliable and responsible, always first on deck and last to
leave, and a glutton for work. His coming with us, which I felt to be
essential, meant a later start than I had bargained for since, owing to
exams, he would not be available until 10th June. This would certainly
lessen our chances of reaching Ellesmere Is. Its south coast, which was
the only part we could hope to reach, lies as far north as 76° N. It is a
big island, extending north to 83° N., a fact which made it a favoured
jumping-off place for attempts on the North Pole, in particular Peary's
successful attempt in 1909. Parts of the island attain to 5000 ft. though
there are no mountains of a character that would attract a climber; for
me the lure lay in its remoteness and comparative inaccessibility for
a small boat. It had been our objective in 1972 when as a result of *Sea
Breeze* breaking her boom when still 300 miles east of C. Farewell our
plans had to be changed with ultimately disastrous consequences. It
is some 800 miles north of Godthaab and since the winds up there in
summer are usually light and more often than not from north-east, and
since moreover ice would begin to form early in September, a start in
mid-May would be desirable.

I now had three hands and needed only a fourth who would undertake the job of cooking. To have one man responsible for this all the
time instead of the crew taking it in turns seems to me preferable if not
essential on a long voyage. With everyone having a go, each man trusting to his successor to reduce chaos to order, the galley soon becomes
a hurrah's nest, everything on top and nothing to hand, while what
stores have been used and what remains is nobody's business. On several occasions in the past an advertisement in the Personal Column of

The Times, the column that is used and perused by screwballs and other *lusus naturae*, has proved fruitful. On resorting to it again I found some new rules had been made as to what kind of advertisement qualified for insertion in so distinguished a place. Mine read 'Amateur cook (male) wanted for 4 months voyage' and they told me that this could only appear either in the 'Situations Vacant' column or under 'Holidays and Villas'. The first implied the paying of wages; as for the other, although *Baroque* might be regarded as a sea-going villa I wondered how many would regard cooking in her galley off Greenland as a holiday. Finally, as a concession, not to be regarded as a precedent, my advertisement did at length appear in the Personal Column and after all this bother produced precisely four replies. After they had learnt what was in store for them none of the four showed any further interest.

Similar advertisements in the not so distant past have produced at least a couple of dozen replies including several from women—hence, on this occasion, the stipulation 'male'. A woman in the galley would, I am sure, bring with her a little much-needed sweetness and light but old-fashioned prejudices have not allowed me to move with the times. Besides, there is the uneasy feeling that the Chinese sage may well have been right when he decided that discord is not sent down from Heaven but is brought about by women. Moreover few women have any understanding of duffs, especially if these have to be cooked in a bucket. They don't eat them and can hardly be expected to cook them. For a sea-cook one wants an all-rounder, a comprehensive genius like Alexis Soyer whose book *Gastronomic Regenerator* I have just been read-ing, a man who could dish up a banquet for the assembled crowned heads of Europe, make soup for fifty men at a time in the rigours of a Crimean winter, and find time to invent a stove, the Soyer Stove still used by the army in 1914–18.

About this time Solent Radio asked for an interview, holding out as an inducement that it would surely evoke an overwhelming response from would-be crew. So I reluctantly agreed to undergo this brief, dis-tasteful ordeal and there is no doubt that Solent Radio had at least one listener for soon after I had a letter from a Captain Joslin. He was an ex-Master Mariner, *aetat* seventy, evidently heartily sick of life ashore and withal conveying a hint that he could cook. To ask a Master Mari-ner to ship as cook in *Baroque* seemed to me verging on impudence, but we arranged to meet at Lymington where by now it was time for me to go to start fitting-out. Like master, except that they did not know what they were in for, my dogs had now to face up to four months hard in kennels, and having disposed of them and hopefully locked the front door I went down to Lymington on 21st May. Next day Captain Joslin came over from Winchester to have a look at the boat. It may have been the galley that shook him, for it had not been properly cleaned since the previous voyage, and he finally departed with a slightly reluctant 'No'. But within an hour he was back, having in the interim spoken by telephone with a forceful daughter who had apparently urged him to go. Next day he started work on the galley. His age naturally gave me pause, for although I could give him several years he had not been accustomed to small boat voyages in rude climates.

He looked a little frail but I assumed that if he did not thrive he would at any rate survive and I liked the idea of having on board a professional seaman to show how things should be done. Before we parted that evening he mentioned that he was due for a medical check. I feared the worst. Sure enough, two days later he rang to say he would have to cry off. Far from recommending a long sea voyage his doctor had firmly told him to stay at home.

Andrew, whom I kept informed of the state of play, posted a notice in some of the London colleges. This produced quite a few enquiries, mostly from those who would not be available until mid-June. Two who would be free in time I invited down to Lymington that first weekend when there were three tons of pig-iron ballast waiting to be tarred. On this test one of them scored only low marks but the other I rather took-to, a twenty-seven-year-old Dane who had spent a short time in Greenland running the airport hotel at Sondre Stromfjord. He had a care-free attitude, smoking cigars while he wielded the tar-brush. Unluckily he had first to go to Denmark to settle some private affairs and the affairs seem to have settled him. He wrote to say he would be unable to come.

Meantime, the cook problem still unsolved, we got on with the fitting out. Something could still be hoped for from those fickle allies time and chance, but with sailing day provisionally fixed for 5th June time was running out. Having set up the ratlines I could go aloft to hang the blocks for the throat and peak halyards and the strops and blocks for the jib and stays'l halyards. An elderly bystander reproved me for not leaving this to the young crew. John happened to be one of those unfortunates with no head for heights and never succeeded in reaching the crosstrees, while had it been left to Nicholas I should have had to listen to a steady, unstoppable flow of questions, suggestions, and doubts about the possibility of whatever was in hand. While I was busy aloft the boys were stowing the ballast. Simon Richardson, who had been mate on *Baroque*'s first voyage, had got this for me from a Portsmouth scrap yard, all in handy sizes, nothing heavier than forty pounds. A few pieces were in the shape of the weight on a lead-line with an eye at one end, and when we lost our seven-pound lead, the line parting, we used one of these cut in half as a replacement. It did not take long to stow the ballast. Owing to her harder bilge, finer garboards, and a liberal use of concrete there seemed to be much less room for ballast than in either *Mischief* or *Sea Breeze*.

    This done we could ship the spars—bowsprit, boom, gaff—and bend on the mains'l, and still had plenty of time for painting and varnishing. With praiseworthy zeal John and Nicholas scraped the whole of the capping rail down to bare wood—a long job—before varnishing it. Having sacrificed our big fisherman type anchor the previous voyage we acquired an equally heavy one which was lying rusty and forlorn under my store. According to the yard's oldest inhabitants it had once belonged to *Mischief*. Although it was rusted almost solid we managed to free the stock and when chipped and painted it looked as good as new. The cable, too, had to be laid out, cleaned up, and the appropriate links painted white at five-fathom intervals. The three of us had therefore plenty to do. Dana, in *Two Years before the Mast*, quotes what he calls the Philadelphia Catechism:

> Six days shalt thou labour and do all that thou art able,
> And on the seventh, holystone the decks and scrape the cable.

Baroque's deck had been painted the previous year and it now had another coat in the hope of making it water-tight, so that we had no use for the holystone that we had used on the deck of *Sea Breeze* which still lay in the store. Holystones come in two sizes. A big one, the Sailor's Bible, which is applied standing up, and a smaller one, the Prayer Book, which is used kneeling.

By 30th May we were still without a cook. A telegram, 'Regret impossible', from the last of my always doubtful reserves had blasted that hope. Thus things looked desperate enough when young John bethought him of a London friend, Alec Ramsay, whom he rang. Alec professed interest and when I spoke to him later he decided to come down next day to look us over. In the end he agreed to come and promised to join on 4th June, giving himself three days to organise his affairs. He was a professional photographer and an amateur cook with no sea experience whatsoever but once he had got his sea-legs he never looked back. Keeping a close watch on stores and water, he fed us admirably and economically, and even in the most boisterous weather refused to lower his standards. Life's lottery includes a great many blanks but there are yet a few prizes and I regarded Alec's quite fortuitous presence on board as one of them. In his early days I could fault him on only one count, a strange reluctance or shyness in the matter of duffs. We were thirty-six days out and west of C. Farewell before, as it were, we struck pay-dirt. One of the spotted dog or dead-man's-leg variety, boiled in a cloth and bent at both ends to fit the pan, at last made its appearance. After that, as if a spell had been broken or a curse lifted, we had two a week, cooked in a more refined way in a basin instead of a dishcloth, and each better than the last.

On 1st June the stores came and were stowed, anything that was not in tins or jars—sugar, flour, dried fruit, etc.—being put first in heavy-duty plastic bags. As most of these had originally contained insecticide or fertiliser one had to be a little careful. For the first time we had to go without dried egg, none being obtainable. This is a useful ingredient for cakes, duffs, pancakes and such like, and in the form of omelettes or scrambled eggs, provided it is well laced with Tabasco sauce, makes a welcome breakfast change from porridge. We also took on the usual twice-baked bread, twenty-four loaves of it, and by an oversight a little of it remained when we returned to Lymington in September, on the hard side but still in prime condition and free from mould. Fresh bread will last only ten days or so at the outside before going mouldy so this twice-baked bread sees us through to Greenland where one can get black bread with its superior keeping qualities. In a vegetable locker on deck we had a hundredweight of potatoes and a half of onions. Alec used onions almost daily for cooking and we ate them raw for lunch, yet this half-hundredweight lasted and kept so well that at the end of the voyage there were quite a few left for me to take home.

With Alec's joining on the evening of 4th June the crew, against all the odds, was complete except for the absent Andrew then undergoing the torture of examinations. We had arranged to pick him up at Castletown in Bantry Bay where we would already have put a few hundred miles of westing behind us. Giving Alec a day's grace to accustom himself to the boat I put sailing day back to the 6th June. Having regard to the haphazard way in which they had been gathered together the crew proved to be a great deal better than I deserved. They accepted with equanimity the occasional peevishness of their ageing skipper and the far from occasional dampness of their quarters, doing all that was required of them with unfailing cheerfulness and willingness. Above all they got on well together and when not occupied with work or sail changing contrived to keep themselves amused—chess, Scrabble, even Monopoly for which John contrived a board. They spent much time, too, in argument and debate in which John and Nicholas were eminently vociferous, Alec quieter but equally fluent, and Andrew, who like Moses was very meek, putting in occasional soothing words. Inarticulate and hearing little, I took no part in these debates, but I gathered that in some respects John was almost as much of a Col. Blimp as I was and that Nicholas was against the Establishment or indeed any establishment. Besides his strident debating powers, Nicholas, our bird-man, had a habit of whistling or breaking into loud song, apparently involuntarily, whether on deck or below. Like the poet Gray who could stand only the hissing of the tea-kettle, I am averse to noise. It was like living in the monkey-house or an aviary, an aviary devoted mainly to the keeping of whooping cranes, whistling ducks, and macaws. However, we are all as God made us, some of us much worse, and he who will have eggs must bear with cackling.

CHAPTER VIII

BANTRY BAY AND THE ATLANTIC

H AVING FILLED UP WITH WATER and fuel and, as one hoped, in all respects ready for sea, on the morning of Friday 6th June we cast off and motored down the river. *Baroque's* curious behaviour under power on her first voyage still haunted me. With the engine going she had always refused to turn to port and the only way of overcoming the effect of the offset propeller was to put the engine in neutral. On the second voyage she behaved better and we had no occasion to use the drogue which a friend had gone to the trouble of making in order to counteract this awkward tendency. On this third occasion going down the river my fears were soon forgotten, for she steered almost normally. Perhaps the rough treatment of those two voyages had ironed some kinks out of her hull. We went down to the Needles under mains'l and stays'l and set the jib when outside. I cannot remember ever making a kindlier start in more benign weather, yet with the Needles still in sight astern Alec and Nicholas were communing with the sea over the rail, the latter not sufficiently overcome to forget to tell us in his querulous voice what he wanted for supper.

John, who was happily immune, provided supper for two, letting his imagination run riot to the extent of opening a tin of bully and boiling some spuds. Alec, refusing to give in, cooked breakfast for us next morning but his frequent, forced visits to the deck while doing so resulted in abominably hard eggs. This quite spoilt my day for I am like the valetudinarian Mr. Woodhouse who held that only an egg boiled very soft is not unwholesome. Having caught a few small mackerel we did better for supper; there were just enough for John and I who were the only ones interested. Happily the placid weather still prevailed. I shuddered to think of the resulting shambles had it been otherwise, with only John and a seasick Nicholas to work the boat, neither of them knowing where gear or tools had been stowed or even what some of the gear was properly called.

By the Sunday evening we were off the Lizard. A slight haze as well as a desire for a quiet night decided me to go south of the Scillies instead of north-about round the Seven Stones light vessel. The night proved quiet enough but did not pass without mishap. Coming on deck at midnight to relieve John I noticed a gaping seam in the mains'l. No one could fail to notice so large a hole but John had not allowed it to worry him and he now suggested that we should roll down a few reefs to hide it, sweeping the mess, as it were, under the carpet. By the time we had the sail down some twelve feet of seam had opened and it took me most of next day to close it. To sew in comfort we had to unreeve the clew earing and unlace the after part of the sail. On a warm and sunny evening, the sewing completed, John and I were hauling out the clew again and having something of a struggle as it needs to be bar taut. Francis Bacon, philosopher and essayist, remarked on the pleasure of watching a battle from a distant hill, and Nicholas, watching our struggles as he reclined on a mattress spread on the counter did not forget to ask if he was in the way.

The thickening fine-weather haze prevented our seeing anything of the Scillies or the Bishop Rock, but we were well to the south and could afford to start steering north-west for Bantry Bay where we were obviously going to be late for our rendezvous with Andrew. By the 11th, the appointed day, we were still seventy miles away with the wind blowing directly from where we wanted to go. Tacking, as we now had to do, emphasised once again another curious feature of *Baroque*. Most boats when on the wind under all plain sail will carry some weather helm, that is to say they tend to come up into the wind so that the tiller has to be kept up (towards the wind) to hold the boat straight. On the port tack, the wind blowing from the port side, *Baroque* conformed to this rule, while on the starboard tack she needed a lot of lee helm to keep her up to the wind. In her old age she is evidently beginning to stoop or droop to one side, for what little I have gathered of her past life does not account for her vagaries, it only makes it the more surprising that she is still afloat. Recently a friend sent me a long article on Bristol Channel Pilot Cutters by B. R. Waite which had appeared in the *Yachting Monthly* in 1927. *Baroque* figures prominently in this with two pictures of her. At the end of the article is a list of eighteen Pilot Cutters which had been converted into yachts. Neither *Mischief* nor *Sea Breeze* are listed and many others must have been omitted because the whole fleet, some sixty in all, was sold after the First War when the pilotage went over to steam. According to this article, when the pilots owned and sailed them, the mast was supported only by the shrouds, no backstays at all; nor did they have a bobstay or any bowsprit shrouds; and it was the considered belief of the pilots that since their conversion to yachts, the vessels had lost a great deal of their speed owing to additions to the standing rigging and the fitting of rigging screws in place of deadeyes and hemp lanyards. The picture of *Baroque* confirms the absence of backstay, bobstay, and bowsprit shrouds. The paragraphs referring to *Baroque* are worth quoting in full; the *Saladin* mentioned, her rival, was one of the full-bodied type like *Sea Breeze* and *Mischief*, and had a displacement of thirty-five tons against *Baroque*'s thirty-two tons:

> The difference of the under-water sections of *Saladin* and *Baroque*, as shown in the accompanying photographs, so interested the owners of the two craft that they arranged a friendly race. *Saladin* with her full forward sections proved to be appreciably the faster off the wind. On the wind there seemed to be little difference, and as *Baroque* was handicapped by the drag of a propeller, was the smaller of the two, and had a suit of well-worn winter sails bent, honours to windward might be considered equal. It is interesting to note that *Baroque* is not fitted with runners, where *Saladin* had all the runners and backstays usually carried by yachts. Whether *Baroque* proved her rival's equal to windward by virtue of the play allowed her gear or to her hard bilge and finer garboards forward is difficult to say, but *Saladin*'s superior speed off the wind seems undoubtedly due to her clean run.
>
> *Baroque* is a particularly interesting example of these craft. Built for the pilot service by Hambley in 1902 she was sold when the service was disbanded and eventually found her way to Scarborough where owing to bad times she was left in the harbour to be sold for what she would fetch. Her present owner found her with a large hole in her planking through which the tide ebbed and flowed at will. Except for the hole in her side she was found to be sound so she was put ashore, thoroughly overhauled, one of her engines

removed (her previous owner had installed two) and now has her headquarters at Hamble, from where she cruises winter and summer. She is an extremely comfortable and able craft, and has been fitted up internally by her owner who has made an excellent job of her accommodation.

The mention of *Baroque*'s propeller implies that this race took place when she was no longer a working boat and had been converted to a yacht. Poor *Baroque*! I have already recorded how she was fished up out of Cowes harbour and here she is again full of sea water at Scarborough. Not to mention the two engines inside her and the structural upheaval that these must have occasioned. Where I willingly agree with the writer of this article that she is an able boat, his remarks about her comfort and the excellent accommodation are questionable. Much depends on what you want to accommodate and, of course, since the writing of that article in 1927 she must have suffered many chops and changes at the hands of various whimsical owners. The Registry that I now have goes back only to 1951 and since then she has changed hands no less than eight times. And what a mixed lot these various owners have been—a consulting surgeon, a seaman, a banker, a blacksmith's striker, a plumber, a spinster, a horticulturist—any or all of whom may have wrought drastic changes in her either on deck or below, particularly the blacksmith's striker.

In anticyclonic weather, pleasant enough but inimical to progress, the wind light at north-west with patches of fog, two more days passed until at last late on Friday 13th June we secured alongside at Castletown. Fishing boats, mostly engaged in salmon-netting, left us little room, and my inexperienced crew, trying to pass warps ashore in bundles, did not show up very well. Andrew, who for two days had been playing Sister Anne with the harbourmaster, came down at 10 p.m. with his gear and I was mightily relieved at this reinforcement. The crew went ashore, as they said, for a 'short walk', and announced their return at 2 a.m. by jumping on to the deck from what sounded like a great height. Our sensitive poet Gray would not have liked this, nor did the skipper.

In the morning we had to move to make room for a Spanish trawler and we lay at close quarters stern to stern. Between us a small boat with an outboard engine came in to fill up with petrol from a drum on the quay, and at the same time the Spaniard decided to give his propeller a whirl. Pandemonium! The small boat shot out seawards in a cloud of petrol and our stern did its best to follow, the stern warp having parted. In the afternoon the Spaniard repeated the performance, *fortissimo* and more prolonged. One by one all our warps parted except the bow line. With Andrew busy on the quay retrieving broken warps I was alone on board wondering what Hornblower would have done if the quivering bow-line parted. The rest of the crew were amusing themselves ashore. Like some of my past crews they tended to regard a boat as a car, a necessary evil for getting from one place to another which, on arrival, one parked and forgot about. This time the Spanish bosun, recognising our plight, brought some of his men to our assistance and with a running commentary of what must have been seamanlike Spanish oaths soon had things under control. We made ourselves fast once more as far as possible from Spain.

Having filled up with water we sailed that evening and met some roughish weather outside. Squalls of force six continued throughout the night and most of the following day. None of the crew felt at all happy except John who in an excess of zeal fell into the drink. By sailing too close to the wind he had let the boat go about Chinese fashion and while I was gybing her back and he was getting in the main sheet he fell over the side. He had a hold on the life-rail, thank Heaven, and was able to drag himself back, for the rest of the crew were in no condition to respond smartly to any 'Man Overboard' drill. On one of the voyages south in *Mischief* one of the crew fell overboard while skylarking and it took a good twenty minutes to recover him. We were south of the Cape Verde Is. running under twin staysails so that these had to come down before anything could be done. The man had got into the lifebuoy we had thrown after him but we had gone so far before we were able to start back towards him that we had great difficulty in keeping him in sight. The answer is to keep on throwing things overboard until the boat has been turned round, like laying a trail. On the only other man overboard incident, also on a voyage south in *Mischief*, the victim never had a chance, and why or how he came to go overboard is still a mystery. David Shaw, an officer on leave from the Royal Mail line, had the 6 a.m. to 8 a.m. watch, and when I came on deck before breakfast at about 7.30 a.m. I found the boat on course, the helm lashed, and no helmsman. From the reading on the patent-log it seemed that it had stopped rotating soon after 6 a.m. and on hauling in the log-line we found that it had broken well short of the rotator. Assuming that it had been broken by David grabbing hold of it, he had been in the water well over an hour and must have been a good four miles back. The weather was by no means bad but there were enough white horses to make it difficult to spot anything small. For two hours we sailed back on a reciprocal course, the crew up the shrouds on the look-out. After that we motored back along the course in zig-zag fashion and in fact went on searching until almost sundown. The water was warm and even without a lifebuoy a man might keep afloat for a long time and although the chances of our spotting him were remote it was not pleasant to think that he might well have seen *Mischief.* David Shaw was my key-man, while the rest of the crew, as events soon showed, were one and all what my New Zealand friends call pikers.

Crossing the North Atlantic from east to west is generally uphill work, a fight to make westing. The desired course for C. Farewell is about W.N.W. With a south-west wind we could just about lay the course while winds with a more westerly component, which were also more frequent, pushed us off course to the north. The perfect summer of 1975 enjoyed at home will long be remembered and it might be thought that the same warm, calm conditions would prevail well out into the Atlantic if not right across it; whereas once west of Ireland we ran into typical Western Ocean weather, no better and no worse than on many previous voyages. June is one of the quietest months and on five days the wind reached force seven, there were five days of rain or drizzle, and an equal number of foggy days. Midsummer day was a bright exception, warm, cloudless, windless, with all hands except the skipper bathing over the side. The weather we experience is seldom so widespread as we tend to think, a fact that should worry (though it never does) those who believe in and talk of 'Equinoctial' gales. Within a day or so of the Equinox one observer to his great satisfaction experiences a gale just as he had foretold, while another 200 miles away and an equally convinced believer, has his hopes or expectations dashed by a flat calm.

All these minor prophets who tell us what things will be like fifty years hence, or even next year, should try their hands at the weather which happily enough still remains fairly unpredictable except perhaps for the next twenty-four hours. Two hundred miles or so west of Ireland one is out of the region covered by the Shipping Forecast and by that time anyway our small receiving set could no longer pick up the B.B.C. The Atlantic Weather Bulletin which covers as far as 40° W. is broadcast by W/T and even if we could have picked it up we had no one on board good enough at Morse. With the aid of the barometer and the appearance of the sky, particularly at dawn and sunset, a man does his own forecasting and unless the presages of good or evil are glaringly obvious he seldom gets it right. Some dispense even with a barometer and certainly Joshua Slocum, the first single-handed circumnavigator, had no such thing on board *Spray*. A man like Slocum, though, would be eminently weatherwise, having spent many years as a master in sail where the vessel's safety or at least the safety of her sails and spars depended on the master's ability to read the signs aright. When Nicholas succeeded in wrecking our barometer so that it fell thirty millibars and refused to move, I felt deprived of help as well as annoyed. No doubt in time I should have got used to its absence but in fact it staged a slow recovery by itself without any tinkering on our part.

CHAPTER IX

TO GODTHAAB

A S A SEA-GOING CROW WOULD FLY it is only about a thousand miles from Bantry Bay to C. Farewell. *Baroque* logged 1300 miles and took twenty-four days over it, during which we suffered the usual minor mishaps. Another seam opened in the mains'l, outdoing the first one in length, and since the sail had to be opened out to get at the seam, sewing could only be done in calm spells when the sail lay quiet. There may be some reason for the cloths of a mains'l to be sewn together horizontally rather than vertically (*Mischief*'s mainsails were all made up this way by a very well known sailmaker) but if they are I should like to see them sewn with sinews, preferably those of an elephant, instead of with seaming twine. A tear in the jib was more serious. While handing the sail the crew made a nonsense and got it wrapped round the bobstay. When finally recovered it looked as if it had been caught up in some machine, the clew and part of the sail in ribbons. At first sight I thought it beyond repair but down in the cabin we pieced it together and with two or three of us stitching away for two days it began to look like a sail; by the time we had reinforced it with crude strips of canvas it was nearly as strong as ever, and for the rest of the voyage, though we had to nurse it a little, we had no more trouble. Then we had sanitary problems. The outlet pump on the lavatory broke down and, as we soon discovered, *Baroque* is not well adapted for business over the side. The guard rails finish well short of the counter so that there is nothing there to hang on to and forward of that the double guard rails made things difficult except for a contortionist. Working up till midnight Nicholas and Andrew repaired the pump. At Godthaab I bought a galvanised bucket in case it happened again.

Although another coat of deck paint had been lavished on her the boat appeared to me to be no drier than the previous year, in other words she was just as wet, the drips from the beams persisting insidiously, difficult to trace to their source. As the Tibetans say, one can live comfortably even in hell if one knows how to go about it, and we all devised our own irrigation or anti-irrigation systems based on plastic sheeting and drawing pins. There were other sources probably besides the deck, for in rough weather she needed a lot of pumping. On 28th June when it blew hard out of a clear sky we had to double the watch at night with one man attending to the pump. Otherwise the man coming off watch, whose normal duty it was to clear the bilge, would have spent a lot of time doing this before he could get his head down. Next morning, the wind as fresh as ever, a wave pushed in one of the windows on the port side of the dog-house. In accordance with Sod's Law I had just come off watch and having taken off my oilskins was writing up the log on the chart table inside the dog-house. The log book as well as the chap writing in it got soaked. We boarded over the windows and I removed everything of moment like the navigational books to the bookshelf in the cabin which remained uniquely dry. The following morning, the same wind still blowing, a wave broke the after window on the same side. As the door of the 'heads' was not really needed we used that to put over both the broken windows where it fitted snugly. Shortly afterwards we hove-to and a sight that I got later put us forty miles north of our dead-reckoning position, the effect of leeway after three days of strong W.S.W. winds. Although still 400 miles east of C. Farewell we were in 59° 30′ N. or almost on the latitude of the cape.

The wind continued unfavourable. By going on the starboard tack to gain southing we should also lose ground to the east and that went against the grain. The *Pilot* recommends keeping seventy miles south of C. Farewell, mainly to avoid meeting icebergs, and on all five previous voyages there had been little difficulty in so doing. On only one voyage had we sighted any ice and that when we were closing the land a little west of the cape. Several days of either fog or rain were a hindrance to precise navigation but on 8th July I reckoned we were fifty miles west of the cape and only a few miles south, and that afternoon we sighted a line of what looked like heavy pack-ice about two miles to the north. With the wind light we could just point W.S.W. and on that course we soon found ourselves among scattered floes. So we started the engine and steered due south expecting to be very soon clear of the ice. Not a bit of it. Twenty-four hours elapsed before we won clear and that at the cost of two sprung planks.

By supper time (fried rice and apple crumble) when we stopped the engine, we were still surrounded by floes, no wind to speak of and foggy. After supper we resumed motoring. We must have done nearly twenty miles under the engine and had we but stuck firmly to a southerly course we might have got clear. Instead we tended inevitably to take the line of least resistance, steering towards where the floes appeared most widely scattered, and this was generally to the west. The crew enjoyed the novelty of steering through ice and they were getting plenty of practice. However, towards midnight Andrew cut things too fine, misjudged the distance between two floes, and gave poor *Baroque* a terrible wallop forward of the shrouds on the port side. With the cabin sole almost immediately awash it was clear we had suffered some damage and it did not take long to find that a plank had been sprung about a foot below the water-line forward of the galley. With canvas, a board, and a great many nails Nicholas and Andrew soon reduced the flow to a trickle and we restarted the engine.

By 4 a.m. the floes were far enough apart for us to cut the engine and set all plain sail, and when I took over from John at 6 a.m. of a wonderfully clear, cloudless morning we were cruising along nicely over a perfectly calm sea. Unfortunately we were cruising westwards for all along our port hand, not more than fifty yards away, lay a wall of closely packed ice. Fine on the port bow and about forty miles away the mountains near C. Farewell showed blue in the early morning light, and to the north as far as one could see there were neither floes nor bergs to break the wide expanse of free and open sea. We had met no icebergs among the floes and now the absence of any in sight to the north was very curious, for one expects to see bergs rather than floes anywhere within seventy miles of C. Farewell. Pleasant sailing though it was on this fresh morning I had not been long at the tiller, enjoying the distant mountain prospect, before it occurred to me that we were wasting our time. Seen from the crosstrees the horizon is distant only some six miles; in the absence of a helicopter or a man-lifting kite one could not be sure, but it was highly probable that the ice on our port hand would not diminish to the west and that there would be ice close to C. Farewell and all along the coast to the west. The temptation of proceeding direct to the cape through apparently open water had to be resisted and I soon decided that the safest plan would be to sail east. We therefore went about and began to retrace our steps of the previous day.

Since our return the Meteorological Office have sent me a plot of the ice limits at this time, between 7th and 10th July, which shows the ice extending to some sixty miles east of Cape Farewell and nearly 100 miles to the south. The following long extract from the *Arctic Pilot* explains the ice conditions off the cape:

> Ice is brought down the east coast of Greenland to C. Farewell in the East Greenland current, and subsequently carried west of that cape by the West Greenland current. This ice was called the East Ice by the nineteenth century whalers to distinguish it from the West Ice of Baffin Bay. The Artic pack forming the East Ice is called Storis literally 'large ice', by the Danes. It consists of very old floes, the last remnants of much larger ones originally formed in the Arctic Ocean and there increased to great thicknesses by rafting, up to 100 ft. or more. On the long passage down the East coast the process of weathering and erosion by the sea continues, and by the time the storis reaches C. Farewell the original great floes have been broken up into small irregular ones which are frequently high. Sea erosion has hollowed them out at the water-line, often leaving long rams projecting below the surface. Many of the floes are of fantastic shapes. The majority have a total thickness of up to 20 ft.; these float with from 3 to 4 ft. above the surface. Some, however, stand higher out of the water, from 8 to 10 ft. and occasionally 12 ft. The total thickness of these is estimated to be from 30 to 40 ft.

> The amount of storis which rounds C. Farewell varies in different years and there are irregularities in its rate of movement and in the times of the beginning and ending of its passage past that cape. The rate of the East Greenland current seldom exceeds one knot and wind influence in opposition to the current may be strong enough to check the flow of ice or even for a time reverse it to a northerly direction. The main mass of the storis, consisting of large, thick floes, usually passes C. Farewell in April, but may be delayed until May. Off the south-west coast of Greenland the ice normally reaches furthest north in May, the northern limit being in the vicinity of Fiskernaes. Occasionally, in a heavy storis year, scattered floes

drift as far north as Godthaab in May to August, and rarely, as in 1898 and 1940, even further north. In a light ice year the storis may not reach further north than C. Desolation, 140 miles north-west of C. Farewell.

The amount of ice passing C. Farewell is usually less in June and decreases rapidly towards the end of July. The flow usually ceases in the early part of August. From September to the beginning of next season's flow of storis, no appreciable amount of pack-ice passes C. Farewell in average years, though occasional scattered floes may be met. Every storis floe that passes C. Farewell ends by melting in the relatively warm water of the southern approaches to Davis Strait. As it rounds the C. Farewell region the storis spreads out to the southward to an average distance of 60 to 70 miles in April and May. It has been known to extend from 100 to 150 miles south of the cape. In general, the further the distance from the coast, the greater is the degree of scattering of the ice, but at any given distance the amount of scattering will depend on the total quantity of ice rounding the region of the cape at the time.

The main flow of bergs from the glaciers on the east coast of Greenland round C. Farewell occurs from April to August inclusive, the maximum number being usually in April with a gradual decrease from May to August. Off the cape several hundred large bergs have been reported in sight from a ship at one time. In autumn the number of bergs in this region decreases rapidly, and in winter the vicinity is more or less free from bergs, though occasional ones may be met in any month. The bergs are carried northward and north-westward by the West Greenland current. They end by melting in the central part of Davis Strait, the waters of which are relatively warm, so that no berg from East Greenland ever reaches the Great Bank of Newfoundland and the main transatlantic shipping tracks. The region in which bergs may be met off southern Greenland is much more extensive than that occupied by the storis, and no definite southerly limit can be given. The greatest distance at which bergs are met south of C. Farewell usually occurs in April and May; this is generally up to about 130 miles, but in 1922 bergs extended to 150 miles south of the cape. In April bergs may be found as far to the eastward as 60°N., 32°W.

All that morning we steered east or south-east among floes so thinly distributed that we sailed more or less unhindered. We expected soon to be in the clear and were disconcerted when the floes began to increase rather than diminish in numbers. By noon we had to hand the sails and revert to the engine and an hour later, patience now wearing thin, we still had to pick our way through narrow leads with no signs of any easier conditions ahead. But then from up the mast came the report of open water to the south and when I went up to have a look I saw an abrupt edge to the ice barely half a mile away and beyond it open water with never a floe in sight. A tenuous lead promised to take us a good part of the way but closer to the edge even the eye of faith could discern no opening at all. Had there been any pronounced ice edge the day before we would have shyed away from it, but we had been drawn among floes almost imperceptibly and I expected to emerge from it in the same way. Given the patience to carry on eastwards for a few more hours we might have done so but the sight of open water so close at hand was too tempting. At least we could have a look.

From up the mast it had been clear that we should not escape without a struggle and when we were within two to three hundred yards of the clean-cut ice-edge the struggle began. The narrow lead had petered out. More than that, it had closed in astern of us, providing us thus with at least an excuse for pushing on and for the vigorous tactics that this entailed. Where two floes were far enough apart to accept *Baroque*'s stem we nosed her in, and then with boathooks pushed one or both floes away until she could be squeezed through the gap. The pool beyond would be too small for manoeuvring, and the boat had no steerage way, so her stem would come to rest against the next floe. The crew would then jump on to the ice, push her bows into the nearest gap, and clamber back on board for more business with boathooks. It was all by no means so straightforward and there were times when progress in any direction seemed unlikely. Some floes were on the move, in which case we might get nipped, as we did once at the cost of another sprung plank. Some floes had projecting underwater tongues on which the keel stuck, and since the engine had no power in reverse the crew had to warp her off by hauling from the ice. An observer of the scene would have wondered what we were playing at and if he were at all apprehensive would have thought, like Brer Rabbit, 'that every minit wuz gwineter be de nex'. The shortest follies are the best but it took us more than two hours to conclude this folly. Fortunately the day was calm and clear. Only at the edge itself were the floes moving up and down in response to a gentle swell, while the several banks of fog that lowered in the distance remained stationary. Having at length got clear and put some water between us and the ice we hove-to for a belated lunch. The crew had done well in this trial of strength and nerve and if they had any doubts about the outcome, as once or twice I myself had, they did not let them appear. I made our position that evening 58° 30′ N., 42° 30′ W. or about eighty miles south-west of Cape Farewell. The reader may think it strange that there are no pictures of this episode, of *Baroque*'s hand-to-hand fight with large chunks of ice. Pictures often tell the story better than the account, especially if the account is written by one with a limited vocabulary, a constrained mode of expression, and little or no imagination. In fact we were all too busy, including Alec, whose photographic talent and equipment outdid that of the rest of us put together; too concerned to get clear before wind or ice movement made things worse than they already were.

July 11th proved to be a day on which a church might have appointed a General Thanksgiving to be read; a church, I mean, such as that adorned by the Rev. Dr. Oppimian who figures in Peacock's novels, not so much as a clergyman but as a high priest of good living, one of whose dictums—'Whatever happens in this world never let it spoil your dinner'—as we have seen, is not always easily obeyed. The continuing fine, calm weather retarded progress as well as giving us a chance to straighten the port side capping rail, pushed inwards by a floe the previous day; also to attend to the new leak which was near the water-line and that much easier to get at. But the real cause for rejoicing was that after thirty-six days at sea a duff at last made its appearance, admittedly a trial shot and, unlike some of Alec's subsequent efforts, not a dish to be eaten on one's knees, but undoubtedly a duff, one of the old-fashioned spotted-dog or dead-man's-leg variety, boiled in a cloth. Its shape lent it added interest. Because the ends had had to be bent to fit the saucepan it looked like a sickle moon rather than the conventional rolling-pin. On most voyages our duffs had been steamed in a basin, or on special occasions in a bucket, so this spotted-dick type presented me with the opportunity to regale the crew with the appropriate story, an unwonted exercise on my part and received by them with respectful laughter. The *dramatis personae* are the skipper, the mate, and the cabin boy of a small trading vessel, all apparently messing together. Such a duff as we had just eaten, though probably straighter, is brought in by the cabin boy, and the skipper, before dividing it up, politely asks him which he prefers, 'Middle or ends, boy?' As every schoolboy knows, or did know, the fag-ends of these spotted-dick duffs are invariably stodgy and devoid of currants, mere congealed suet, so the cabin boy naturally replies, 'Middle, if you please, sir'. Whereupon the skipper, with the explanatory remark, 'Well, me and the mate like ends,' proceeds to cut the thing in half.

For the next few days a lot of fog and little enough wind were our portion, more fog than I have known before in Davis Strait, though it is not to be denied that in summer in these northern latitudes fog is all too frequent. Like the sound of breakers, we kept hearing the growl of pack-ice to the north-west and owing to the presence of this ice the sea temperature was still only 2° C. On 14th July, when according to my hopes we should have been in Godthaab, we relished for the first time what I call a 'Greenland day', a pale blue cloudless sky and a vivid blue sea flecked here and there with dazzling white floes and bergy bits. We were only some thirty miles off the coast and so getting a useful lift from the current which follows the trend of the coast to the north-west. We saw our first icebergs, met an occasional trawler, and could obtain a rough check on our progress by the ice-blink reflected from the Frederikshaabs glacier with its ten-mile wide front. The glacier extends thirty-five miles inland and rises to a height of 6000 ft. The trawlers were engaged in salmon netting rather than trawling. According to a skipper we met at Holsteinborg the cod and halibut, owing to a fall in sea temperature, have deserted the banks which extend far up the west coast and which up to a few years ago were rich fishing grounds. On earlier Greenland voyages we used to see not only dozens of trawlers fishing these banks but also the three-masted Portuguese schooners anchored on one or other of the banks with their dories (sixty to each schooner) spread far and wide busy hand-lining for cod. Nowadays, as we learnt to our cost on *Baroque*'s first voyage, almost any fishing vessel one meets is either laying or standing by to haul in a half-mile long

salmon net. Two days before reaching Godthaab we narrowly escaped
an entanglement with a net such as had happened on the first voyage.
I had the 6 a.m. to 8 a.m. watch on a perishing cold morning, thick fog
and a biting north-east wind, the air temperature 2° C. When an ice-
berg loomed up I had to alter course smartly and passed within feet of
a dan buoy at the windward end of a salmon net. Even in fog one can
generally spot a berg in time to sheer away but a dan buoy, which is
merely a pole with a small flag supported by a float, is another matter.
Shortly after we met an Italian vessel *Ave Maria* at anchor, with one of
her boats out busy laying buoys all over the place. Whether these were
for nets or for some more obscure purpose we could not decide.

My flawless 'Greenland' days were notably scarce at this time
when, if it were not foggy, it would be either raining or blowing. Early
on the 19th it blew so hard that we had three rolls in the mains'l. Had
the whole sail been up things might have been worse, for bird-man
Nicholas chose that moment to execute an imperial Chinese gybe,
his second. On this occasion the boom crashed over with enough violence to break the block and spread the hook of the backstay tackle.
Normally when gybing the main sheet is hauled in until the boom is
almost amidships before it is allowed to go over, whereas in an acciden-
tal gybe it slams over of its own accord and the violence with which it
fetches up against the first obstruction, either the backstay or the main
shrouds, depends upon how much of the main sheet is out and the
strength of the wind. Chinese gybe, I suppose, referred originally to
the way a Chinese junk would gybe, that is to say all standing, for with
no heavy boom and the weight of the sail spread evenly by the bat-
tens with which it was fitted, this could be done with impunity. Among
yachtsmen now it has a derisory meaning, an unseamanlike or lub-
berly performance by the helmsman, for which there is sometimes an
excuse and sometimes not. For instance, an excessively heavy roll may
make a gybe almost unavoidable especially with a gaff mainsail. To
Englishmen there is, or at any rate used to be, nothing funnier than a
foreigner, so that 'Chinese gybe', like other similar expressions, may be
just a sailor's way of ascribing to foreigners anything ludicrous or lub-
berly. For something that has been forgotten we have 'left behind, like
the Dutchman's anchor', or 'Dutchman's cape' for non-existent land,
'Irish pendants' for unwhipped rope's ends, and 'Paddy's hurricane'

for a flat calm with the wind blowing vertically upwards. The Chinese crop up again in the expression 'twelve knots and a Chinaman'. Before the patent log came into use a log-line, log-ship (the piece of wood swimming upright at the end of the line), and a sand-glass were the means of ascertaining the vessel's speed. The line was divided by knots, usually twelve, each knot about forty-seven feet from the next for a twenty-eight-second sand-glass. One man held the reel from which the line ran out, another tended the line, and an officer watched the sand-glass, and as soon as this ran out the line was checked and the number of knots that had been reeled off gave the speed of the ship. When doing more than twelve knots the man holding the reel was in peril. Apparently in one of the famous flyers of the last century her speed was such that when the line ran out the man holding the reel—a Chinaman, of course—was jerked overboard and lost. So that a vessel doing more than her normal speed—*Baroque*, for instance, doing seven knots and trembling with excitement at that—might be reported as doing 'twelve knots and a Chinaman'.

After this damaging gybe we lay-a-try for most of a day of continuous rain with wind gusting to force eight. By evening it had moderated and we started closing the land towards Godthaab fjord which I reckoned lay thirty miles to the south-east. At 10 p.m. we sighted the lighthouse on one of the numerous outlying islands. Lighthouses in Greenland are few and far between, existing only at the entrances of the busier ports. They are modest structures with equally modest lights—the Godthaab light, for instance is in a twenty-three foot high cement tower. In summer, when the nights are never properly dark, the structure will be made out long before the light shows. We lay off for the night, drifting north, and owing to a combination of baffling winds and batteries that were almost flat we did not make the harbour until late next afternoon.

CHAPTER X

GODTHAAB AND NORTHWARDS

◆

THE HARBOUR THAT LIES some twelve miles up the fjord is now far more commodious than on our first visit in *Mischief* in 1961; indeed there have been further improvements since *Baroque's* first visit in 1973. We had no difficulty in finding a berth at a long, wooden jetty of recent construction for the accommodation of small fishing boats. This now extends almost the whole length of the high rock wall on which the names of numerous visiting ships have been painted. *Mischief* still figures prominently and this time we added *Baroque*. Presumably because they are such rare birds, the Danes take the kindliest possible view of visiting yachts, which is to say that they completely ignore them. Our 'Q' flag could be hauled down forthwith and without waiting for Customs or Immigration officials we were free to stretch our legs on shore. For the 35 days from Ireland we had averaged a pitiful forty-four miles a day and were down to our last gallon of water.

At the main wharf across the harbour they had a large charging plant for keeping the batteries of the fork-lift trucks up to scratch, and the harbour master readily undertook to have our almost flat batteries put on charge. With a borrowed wheelbarrow we took them over. A wet and windy morning turned into an afternoon fine and warm enough to bring out the mosquitoes in some force, but with Godthaab rapidly becoming a concrete jungle they are less numerous than they were. On our first visit the Danish workmen making roads or erecting buildings all wore face veils. We made fruitless attempts to get at the leak on the port side, first by swinging out the boom with the heavy anchor and one of the crew on the end. Then we attached a long warp to the throat halyards and some friendly Danes in a motor boat took the warp and made it fast to a trawler on the far side of the harbour. But our mooring warps—which we could not let go—always prevented our heeling the boat over far enough to bring the sprung plank above water and in the end we gave up and instead put a cement box over the leak inside. What with boulders on the bottom and the absence of any wall to lean against I felt that we might do more harm than good by trying to beach her. Next day, 23rd July, the Danish Royal Yacht came in, on her way to the airport up Sondre Stromfjord where the royal party were to be picked up. Her beautiful appearance was marred by the sloppiness of the crew, most of them with long hair streaming out from under their sailor's caps. The Danish navy, I think, is manned by National Service men serving for only a short time which must embitter the hair question. A man finishing his time with short hair would have to face several months of civilian ignominy before it grew again. The old *Mallemuken*, a small gunboat which I remembered from our 1961 visit, was also in harbour. We had had shower baths on board her—the only place one could get a shower at that time—and even then fourteen years ago, she had looked far from modern. Now there is a fine Sailor's Home down by the harbour where one can get a shower.

The fish factory, the only productive unit, did not appear to be working full time, yet Godthaab continues to grow and even to thrive though it is not easy to see why. New buildings were still going up while the amount of traffic that dashes about is astonishing when one remembers that there are no roads anywhere outside the township; all the cars and lorries were merely going from the harbour to the town or from one street to the next, and there are not that many streets. There is an oasis of peace and quiet round the old harbour which is still used by small fishing boats, their catch going to an adjacent open-air market where, I noticed, you could also buy wild rhubarb and odd bits of meat that might have been whale, seal, reindeer, or even dog. Here, too, are the church, the Hans Egede statue, and his original house built of stone, the only such house in Godthaab. Hans Egede was a Norwegian missionary who came to Godthaab in 1721, half expecting, or at least hoping, to find the Norsemen still there. He started missionary work among the Eskimo, established a commerce with Denmark, and was thus the founder of Godthaab. His son Paul continued the Greenland mission and completed the translation of the New Testament into Eskimo, a task left unfinished by his father who died in 1758.

The Norsemen or Vikings, referred to above, the toughest and most adventurous colonists of all time, are closely associated with Godthaab as well as with south-west Greenland. Eric the Red founded the so-called Eastern Settlement or Osterbygd around Julianehab in 986 A.D. and in time it comprised 300 farms, a cathedral, churches, a monastery and a nunnery. The Vesterbygd or West Settlement around Godthaab was smaller, consisting of some ninety farms and four churches, seventy of the farms have been located. Whether the settlers died out because worsening ice conditions cut off essential supplies from Europe or whether the Eskimo exterminated them is conjectural. The annual Greenland carrier (Knarren) made its last voyage in 1369 and in 1406 the last vessel known to have reached Greenland arrived there by mistake and did not get away for four years. The rest is silence. John Davis, the great Elizabethan seaman-explorer who made three voyages in search of the North-west Passage, was the first European to rediscover Greenland. He visited Godthaab in 1585, had moderately friendly relations with the Eskimo who were then there, and made no mention of any Norsemen. Cape Desolation, north of Julienehaab, was so named by him, also Sanderson's Hope near Upernavik, which was his furthest north: attained on his third Greenland voyage in 1587. On this voyage his eagerness to push north on what might be a fruitless quest had to be reconciled with regard for the pocket of his faithful backer William Sanderson, a London merchant. So he sent his two larger vessels, *Sunshine* and *Elizabeth*, to fish on the Grand Banks while he himself pushed north in *Helen*, a barely seaworthy clinker-built pin-nace of only 20 tons. In 72° 12′ N. they sighted and named the great cliff Sanderson's Hope, seeing, as Davis wrote, 'no ice towards the north, but a great sea, free, large, very salt and blue, and of an unsearchable depth'. But then a north wind drove them west until they encountered the 'Middle Pack' and were forced south.

It was time for us to push on northwards and sight Sanderson's Hope. We sailed on the evening of 24th July and our departure was, as the phrase goes, fraught with anxiety. To get water we went to the main quay whence, as the harbourmaster said, we must leave by 5.30 p.m. to make room for an incoming freighter. Though we needed only 20 gals of fuel the harbourmaster had also arranged for a bowser to come down to the quay to deliver it. At five o'clock, with no sign of the bowser, the light airs of anxiety that were already playing upon the brow of expectation rose to a stiff breeze when a large Danish frigate suddenly appeared at the harbour entrance. I was about to abandon

The main quay at Godthaab, capital of Greenland

our fuel and give the order to cast off when the frigate, instead of making for the quay, let go her anchor in the middle of the harbour. The harbour is small so that she lay not far from the quay. The bowser then arrived and we filled up and paid our bill with about five minutes in hand. We were just moving away from the quay, the engine going, when the bird-man reported no oil pressure and stopped the engine. A slight breeze blowing down the harbour sufficed to fill the stays'l and we managed to swing past the frigate without pranging her with our bowsprit, and without saluting her either, as I suppose we should have done, my *sangfroid* at that moment in abeyance. Hurriedly setting the jib and mains'l we reached the harbour entrance almost at the same time as the expected freighter. Heading as we were for one side of the narrow entrance we had urgent need to go about, but it seemed better to run aground than to be impaled as we crossed the bows of the freighter. We stood on in hope as the distance to the rocks rapidly shortened and put about the moment we had room.

The tide was making and in spite of a fair wind we had gained less than a mile when the wind petered out and a dense fog came down. By this time the engine was in action, the lack of oil pressure having proved a false alarm, and we decided to carry on for the fjord entrance, the course being straightforward. The south side of the fjord is a string of islets and islands which we needed to keep close on our port hand, so that the navigator was considerably perturbed when one of these loomed up to starboard. Navigational errors, if they do not end in disaster, can be laughed off and attributed to unknown currents or acts of God. In this case we were probably set south by the tide. Of such errors, errors on a more sublime though not impossible scale, the Editor of Lecky's *Wrinkles* has a classic remark: 'There is nothing so distressing as running ashore, unless it be a doubt as to which continent the shore belongs.'

Having regained the fairway we groped our way from island to island as each in turn came up out of the fog seldom more than a hundred yards away, ticking them off on the chart as one might the buoys marking a channel. Though many people do not mind or even prefer eating to the sound of what passes for music, few would enjoy eating to the thump of *Baroque*'s engine at close quarters. We usually stopped the engine if motoring and meal-time happened to coincide, but now

There were a few large bergs about, majestically contemptuous of the seas

in fog, close to islands, and a tide running, we had to keep going. This was particularly unfortunate because Alec had chosen to dish up something akin to a banquet—salmon (bought by Andrew) and sauce Hollandaise followed by treacle duff, an invitation to feats of higher gluttony. 'Never let it spoil your dinner', and no doubt that care-free gastronome Dr. Oppimian would not have let a trifle of engine noise spoil his. I am more weak-minded. Noise, fog, and navigational worries altogether spoiled mine, and how glad I was when a little later we picked up the dim light on the outermost island, which in fact showed up rather better in the prevailing gloom of fog and twilight.

Two days of fog and northerly winds were an unusual combination, for it is southerly winds that usually bring fog. This kept us on the starboard tack steering almost due west and in such thick weather we were not sorry to be well away from land. Raw days they were, too, the fog bringing the air temperature down to 4° C. The perfect 'Greenland' day that followed allowed sights to be obtained and these showed that we were a good seventy miles from the coast and thus beyond the influence of the north-going current. Spanish omelette and yet another duff for supper, Alec by now having found them as easy to make as we did to eat. Lay on McDuff, was the word, and even at the rate of two or three a week no one felt like crying, 'Hold, enough'. After another cloudless day we had thirty-six hours of north-easterly wind of nearly gale force. We could make no progress on either tack in such a wind and when a seam went in the mains'l we lay-a-hull, rolling heavily in a short, steep sea. There were a few large bergs about, majestically contemptible of the seas that broke angrily against them. To avoid drifting on to a berg I found that with patience and the tiller hard over *Baroque* could be brought stern on to wind and sea, upon which she soon gathered steerage way and went with increasing speed at a fair lick down wind under bare poles.

Overnight the wind dropped and we enjoyed a warm, windless morning on which to do eight feet of stitching in the mains'l. I also made up some baggywrinkle against an expected visit from Father Neptune, for we were now nearing the Arctic Circle. Still making westing, we were nearly a hundred miles from the coast, rather nearer to Baffin Is. than to Greenland, for hereabouts Davis Strait is only 180 miles wide. C. Dyer and Mt. Raleigh, which we visited and climbed in 1962 were only eighty miles to the west. John Davis had led me to seek out Mt. Raleigh. Nearly four hundred years ago, lying at anchor in Exeter Sound, he recorded: 'We lay under a brave mount the cliffs whereof were orient as gold. This mount we named Mt. Raleigh.'

A cold foggy night succeeded this pleasant day, both air and sea temperatures falling to 2° C. To account for the drop in sea temperature from 5° to 2° C. I thought that there must be ice about and sure enough at noon we sighted a line of floes to the west. This was probably remnants of what the whalers used to call the Middle Pack, the great, pear-shaped field of ice that in spring and early summer extends from Baffin Bay down the middle and western half of Davis Strait. Having altered course to E.N.E. we later passed close to more outlying floes and the presence of these together with some fitful sunshine decided me to invite Father Neptune on board forthwith although we were a few miles short of the Arctic Circle. The ice would make a suitable setting for the ceremony.

John came in over the bows stark naked except for the length of baggywrinkle round his waist. The deck broom had been converted into a passable trident, his crown glistened with silver foil, while his beard, also of baggywrinkle, should have lent him a venerable air. In fact it reminded me more of Leech's picture of Facey Romford than of Majesty. I welcomed him on the foredeck with a swig of rum, accepted humbly the scroll he presented (our *laissez-passer*), and turned to address the crew, most of them on their knees busy with cameras. 'Men, As we are now entering His Majesty's arctic domains he himself has graciously come on board to hand us in person the needed documents. Three cheers for His Majesty.' And when the cheers had subsided: 'He orders me to pipe all hands to dance and skylark and to splice the mainbrace.' As John and I had finished our rum we took advantage of this last order to have our glasses recharged. Sausage and mash were, perhaps, an ignoble conclusion to an auspicious day but no such criticism could apply to what followed—a weightily majestic chocolate duff accompanied by a smooth sauce, both, of course, the colour of royal purple.

A sight next day confirmed that we had crossed the Arctic Circle and the air temperature of 1° C. that had been recorded at 6 a.m. was in accordance. A trawler, *Orion Arctic*, had passed in the night. We met

John Shipton, representing Father Neptune, came in over the bows
stark naked except for the baggywrinkle around his waist

her subsequently at Holsteinborg and learnt that she was on charter engaged in seismic survey, not in trawling. The Danish Government had recently allotted blocks off the west coast for oil exploration and Orion Arctic and two other vessels were already so engaged. We were now closing the land north of Holsteinborg, the coast littered with islets of barren rock and backed by snow mountains. On any day but this, a typical 'Greenland' day of brilliant sunshine, such a coast would have looked grim and forbidding but for us it had a warm and friendly appearance. Off this coast is the Great Hellefiske Bank that recently was rich in cod and halibut, the name alone suggesting to anyone as ignorant as myself 'hellish good fishing'. Hereabouts on *Baroque*'s first voyage we were pestered by salmon nets. This year we saw only one net and only two trawlers fishing for those few cod and halibut that had not left for new pastures. When becalmed, we put a line down near the bottom and succeeded in catching a worm, foul-hooked at that.

I had a mind to go through the Vaigat, the sixty-mile long channel between Disko Is. and the mainland. The slight extra distance would be worth incurring for Alec to get some professional studies of ice-bergs, for there is no other place where such majestic monsters can be seen in such great variety and great profusion. As the Pilot remarks: 'In June, after the break-up of the winter ice, thousands of bergs, some of them from 200 ft. to 300 ft. high, drift backwards and forwards with the tidal stream; these bergs render navigation dangerous and safe anchorage almost impossible.' The Jacobshavn Isfjord where two large glaciers descend from the inland ice is the main source of these bergs. In late summer of 1961 in *Mischief* we had passed through the Vaigat southbound, and apart from running aground in fog had encountered no great difficulty. To enter the Vaigat proper we had first to get into Disko Bugt at its southern end and the thirty-mile wide entrance is encumbered by a number of islands. With a fair wind taking us right up to the small island of Rotten it looked like a piece of cake until the wind headed us and began to blow with some strength directly out of the Vaigat. Moreover we were still on the wrong side of the Kronprin-sens Islands, a large group that until recently were known as Whale Fish Islands, a name that stirs the imagination and conjures up visions of the old whaling fleets. Godhavn on Disko Is., ten miles north of the Whale Fish group, was the principal port of call for the whaling fleet on its way north. Anyhow, whatever the name of these islands, the north-east wind stopped us from getting past them. Having tacked several times without gaining much ground we finally bore away to the north-west to go outside Disko Is., foregoing the Vaigat but at least turning a foul wind into a fair wind.

CHAPTER XI

AN ABRUPT CONCLUSION

"There is a world of difference between being outward bound by choice and homeward bound by necessity."

R. T. McMullen, *Down Channel*

By the time we reached the south-west corner of Disko Is., the wind was all over the place and fast dying. A little more patience and we might have been sailing or at any rate motoring through the Vaigat, but whether that would have prevented what was about to happen, or merely deferred it, is conjecture. We handed the sails, the mains'l with two rolls still in, and motored up the west coast of Disko Is. for a couple of hours before stopping for supper. For this kind of yachting, where comfort and the care of the stomach have priority over progress, some wag has recently coined the word 'gastronavigation'. For supper we had potato pie and duff, a little heavy perhaps on the carbohydrates and a meal from which anyone with a keen sense of foreboding might have expected an uneasy night. And so it proved. With no wind we lay becalmed and drifting about two miles offshore, a shore fringed with grounded bergs, until very suddenly at about 1 a.m. the wind came in with considerable violence from south-west. The crew responded smartly. Not only was it a fair wind for making northing but it also put us on a lee shore. Having regard to the strength of the wind the two rolls in the mainsail would be needed. We left them in and swigged up the sail. As the last inches were got out of the throat and peak halyards I began easing out the main sheet whereupon, with no warning, the boom broke clean in two. Had it not been for the sail wrapped round them the two separate pieces might have led us a proper dance. As it was, with a struggle, we soon had the whole lot inboard and secured, and the sail down. Setting the trysail we steered north-west to gain some much needed offing, for a thick drizzle now obscured the coast. To balance the trysail the jib had to come down.

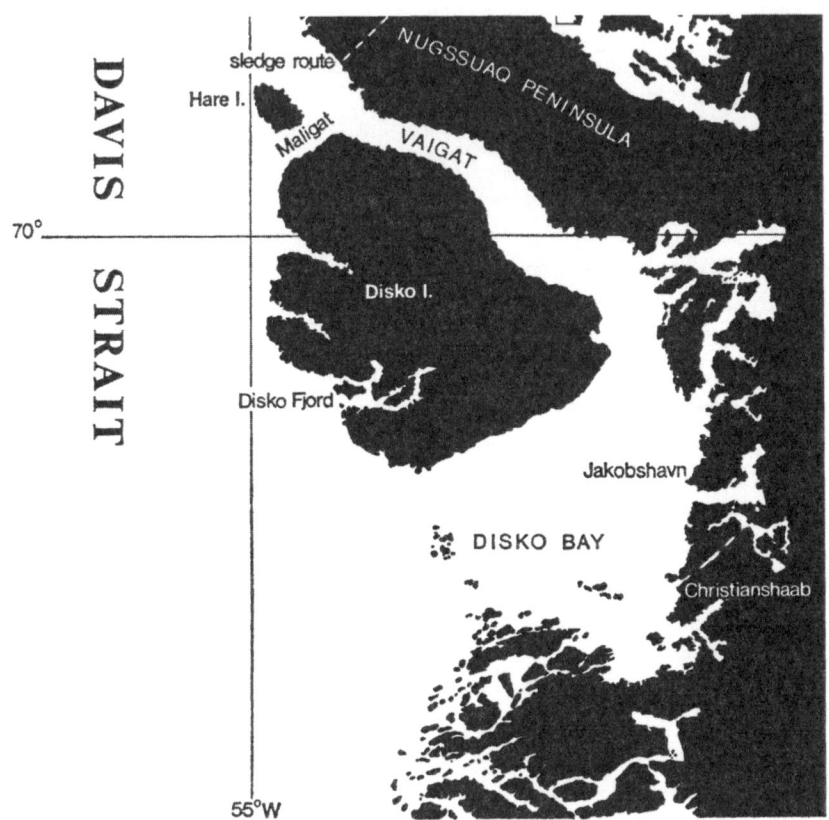

Map 3: The Vaigat and Disko Bay

In the process it went overboard and was recovered badly torn with four feet of the luff wire sticking out. On the whole, a night to be remembered.

By morning I had decided against going any further north. This was 7th August and if we were to be back by the end of September we should have to start for home not much later than mid-August. True we were in only a semi-crippled state. In light winds we could use the mainsail without any boom and we had the trysail, but with that we should make no progress at all against head winds. We were just north of 60° N. Ellesmere Is. was still 450 miles away and Upernavik, which I had rather expected might be our furthest north this voyage, was 250 miles off. Water and food for the passage home could be had at Holsteinborg where there was also a slight possibility of having a boom made; though if that meant a long delay, as it well might, we could manage without. It might be slow work in Davis Strait but once south of C. Farewell the brave westerlies should hustle us along. So, to the disappointment of us all, we put about and headed south-east. Headed is the word, for we were not moving. The wind had gone almost as suddenly as it had come leaving behind a terrible lop in which we lurched and sidled closer to Fortune Bay—a misnomer, I thought—near the southern edge of Disko Island. Lop or no we had to get clear, besides the land, there were icebergs all round and we could see the white water over the sunk rock called Parry's Skaer. Labouring heavily in the confused sea, the propeller at times thrown clear of the water, we motored for two hours.

In recent years I have had no luck at all with spars. *Sea Breeze* broke her topmast, her bowsprit, the gaff twice, and finally the boom. *Baroque* sprung her boom the first voyage, and now the replacement, a hollow spar, had survived only two voyages. Chinese gybes, I suppose, are not conducive to long life in spars, but a boom should be man enough to withstand some occasional ill-treatment. Coming back across the Atlantic on her first voyage in 1956 *Mischief* had sprung her boom, but the replacement which, so far as I remember, was a solid spar and an inch thicker than the original, was still there in 1968 when we lost *Mischief.* It was a spar, I might add, whose size and weight struck terror into all beholders, particularly the crew; but if a man is going to be struck by a boom a little extra weight is neither here nor there, the effect will be equally lethal. Whether there is any real evidence for it—beyond that of my own ill-luck—it has been suggested that Pilot Cutters were liable to break their booms on account of the size of the sail, the length of the boom, and above all their roller-reefing gear. With the sheet made fast to a revolving iron collar at the extreme end of the boom the strain comes on only one point, and the more the sail is rolled the greater becomes the buckling effect as the leech comes further and further inboard. One would have thought that hand-reefing would produce the same effect, the leech, with two or three reefs pulled down, coming equally far inboard. Metal spars break, and anyhow such a spar would be an anachronism in a Pilot Cutter, so the only answer seems to be a solid and thick enough boom. One is reminded of the complaint of James Pigg, Jorrock's North-country huntsman, who when riding half-drunk through a gateway nearly had his leg torn off by one of the gateposts: 'Sink. They dinna make their gates half wide enough.'

Mainly owing to lack of wind the 150 miles to Holsteinborg took us five days. Having unwrapped the mainsail from the boom we lashed the two pieces on deck and used the sail without the boom; but since this imposed a severe strain on the clew of the sail it could be done only in light winds. Nor, without a boom, did the sail prove very effective if the wind was ahead. On the 11th, by dint of much motoring we were near the Qagssit Islands, a group lying just off Holseteinborg. Despite the wonderfully clear, calm evening I decided not to try to find our way in that night, a lucky decision because we were soon enveloped in thick fog. Meantime, with a light Fisherman anchor and two long warps bent together we had anchored in 30 fms., and until the fog came down, from bearings taken to the islands and mountains beyond, we seemed to be holding well in spite of a strong north-going current. Ignorance now indeed proved to be bliss. We spent a quiet, untroubled night and only when the fog lifted, which it did not do until noon next day, did we find that we had drifted three miles north and closer inshore. With nothing to see and nothing to hear the man on anchor watch had no means of telling whether or not we were dragging. Perhaps if we had used the chain, its grumbling as it dragged along the bottom might have warned us. Anchoring with warps in fog, I felt, must be unseamanlike.

We did not get in until late that evening. The marks were not easy to pick up, though the leading lights for the final dog-leg approach to the harbour were very clear. We anchored short of the inner harbour used by small boats and while we were squaring up a young Greenlander who was alongside handed us a freshly caught cod. Andrew, taking the hint, put a line over the side and soon had two more fat cod. Fried cod for breakfast and fish chowder for supper. Going ashore that night for a quick look round I could recognise only the shipyard and the church with the whalebone arch over the gate, so much had the place altered since 1962. The main harbour where we had found barely room or even enough water to anchor has been enlarged and enclosed with wharves, and the beach off which we had lain, where starving huskies waded in search of fish, has disappeared under a road. The shopping centre—for there are now a few shops—is a short half-mile uphill from the harbour, far enough apparently to justify the presence of numerous taxis. In 1962 a taxi might well have been taken to avoid being mauled by the packs of huskies which then roamed everywhere like wolves, licking oil drums and even fishing, for it was the custom then to feed them only in winter when they worked pulling sledges. The Town Council or the local R.S.P.C.A. have applied the screw. The only huskies to be seen were in wire cages outside the Greenlander houses where, one hopes, they are occasionally fed.

Next day, by swinging out the gaff with a weight on the end and bringing some ballast up on deck we canted the boat over far enough to put a tingle over the sprung plank. With no mooring warps to stop her she heeled over readily. An Englishman, a meteorologist from *Orion Arctic* which was now in harbour, paid us a visit. She was a Canadian vessel with a crew of at least half a dozen different nationalities. In contrast to this was the trawler *Greenland*, the crew all Faeroese and the skipper and mate, father and son. The skipper, who spoke excellent English, looked a proper seaman, quite distinct from the son with his spectacles, long hair, and beard. It was this skipper who told us that colder water had driven most of the fish away from the Greenland banks.

We all had showers at the well-run Seaman's Home and I paid a visit to the shipyard. In 1962, and it may be so still, this was the only place in Greenland where a vessel of moderate size could be hauled out. A helpful Dane was running it then and we had had *Mischief* hauled out to see if she had sustained any damage from some ice she had hit. Since then it has been enlarged and seemed to be busy enough with two small trawlers hauled out undergoing repair; moreover from some of the timber lying about I thought a boom could have been made. But even the enquiry stage was never reached. In the Greenlander manager I met a blank wall. We had not a word in common and he showed no interest in the reason for my visit. The same afternoon, having done our shopping (mainly black bread), we went alongside for water, or rather alongside *Greenland*, the nearest we could get to the quay. Before we cast off they gave us two buckets of prawns, not as fresh as one might wish of prawns but fresh enough to eat.

Outside we had a fair northerly wind and a lively following sea. With her nose turned for home *Baroque* thought fit to kick up her heels while the compass behaved even more wildly, trying hard apparently to describe circles. On settling down, as later it did, the direction in which it pointed was obviously suspect. At noon next day with the sun due south the compass also pointed south, whereas with the local magnetic variation of 48° W. the compass should have pointed nearly south-east. We searched carefully to see if there was anything near the compass to account for its behaviour and found nothing. Thereafter, every day we compared the compass with the sun's bearing either at noon or whenever I took a sight and got an azimuth. As one goes south down Davis Strait and then eastwards across the Atlantic the westerly magnetic variation decreases by something like five degrees every 200 miles. Our compass ignored this and continued to point more or less true all the way home. It might well have been a gyro compass. Here was another unsolved mystery of the sea and on our return I consulted a compass adjuster in Southampton who reported:

> I have today tested this compass for friction and period. The compass is not frictional which means the sapphire and pivot are satisfactory. The period was 13 seconds which was exactly the same as the period of a brand new Medina compass from stock. The error which you experienced is indeed very strange and as I understand it, the deviation was always approximately the same amount as the variation

with opposite name so as to give a nil compass error throughout the
return voyage. What caused the deviation to decrease with the variation is mysterious for a wooden boat. Are you sure there is not iron
or steel near the compass position to give an induced effect, or any
electric motor for steering gear, window wipers, clear view screens, or
auto-pilots nearby?

This is not the place to enter into the difference between variation and
deviation, but in wooden boats the latter is usually small and in all
the boats I have had we have ignored it, possibly not justifiably but at
any rate without detriment. As regards the enquiries at the end of this
report I could answer with my hand on my heart that there were no
such things in *Baroque* nor ever likely to be.

Despite a lot of fog we made good progress. By the 17th the log
had clocked up 3000 miles for the voyage, and on the night of the
18th with fog all round and a clear sky overhead we lay becalmed off
Godthaab. Meantime we had been living on the country, or rather the
sea, eating a great many prawns mostly in curries, and now Andrew
contributed to this rich living by catching two nice cod. We were over
the Fyllas Bank and had anchored accordingly to fish. There were evidently still some of the hardier characters around, like the Serpentine
Christmas Day bathers, who did not object to colder water. The fog did
not clear until the following evening, a lovely tranquil evening with
the slowly dispersing fog reluctantly revealing a glorious panorama of
distant mountains. We were still motionless when a local trawler with
a friendly Danish skipper on his way into Godthaab came skilfully
alongside and passed us a line. We had a gam while his Greenlanders
passed over a lot of red fish with big eyes and serrated spine, together
with a huge box of prawns. I gave the skipper a bottle of whisky and,
besides the sea-food, he gave us the latest weather report from Godthaab. It proved, I'm afraid, to be as far out as some of our own. All
hands were busy next morning cleaning prawns and we had our first
go at them for lunch, finding them sweet and tender, far better than
those given to us at Holsteinborg. When we began moving again it was
with the help of a slight breeze from north sent specially by Aeolus not
so much for our benefit but to spite the Godthaab weather boys who
thought it should be southerly force five to six.

For the next few days we continued to make good progress south, pestered though we were by bergs and bergy bits. The weather, too, was generally thick and by now, from 10 p.m. onwards, the nights were dark. Off this part of the coast, midway between Godthaab and C. Farewell, the cold current fans out to the west carrying with it numerous bergs and bergy bits. On the 22nd and 23rd, when we sometimes sighted up to ten bergs in a watch, the sea temperature varied between 5°C. and 2°C. For the next two days with the temperature at 7°C. we saw no bergs and then by steering east, when we got within fifty miles of C. Farewell, the temperature fell again to 2°C. and more bergs were sighted. The last berg was sighted on the 27th August and thereafter the sea temperature rose steadily all the way across the Atlantic. This premature steering eastwards towards C. Farewell was the result of my stupidly toying with the idea of going through Prins Christians sund, the fifty-mile long channel between the east and west coasts just north of C. Farewell. We had been through it from west to east in 1970, but then we were already inshore, knew more or less where we were and where the entrance was. At the eastern end there is a weather station where we had had a royal welcome and been given vast quantities of stores. This, rather than the spectacular scenery of the channel may have been what drew me towards it on this occasion. But the continuing thick weather, the dark nights, the number of bergs about, the strong current inshore, and the difficulty of identifying, among many others, the right fjord, together aroused enough apprehension to overcome my greed. Accordingly we resumed our southerly course. It would have been a difficult undertaking and not altogether prudent.

Even when well away from the coast we had some pretty severe frights during those few days, impressing upon us the difference that the dark nights made, particularly when combined with fog. On the afternoon of the 22nd, in the absence of wind, we had been motoring. By evening a fine north-westerly breeze enabled us to start sailing but brought with it thick fog. Andrew's startled cry brought me on deck at the jump and the brief glimpse I got of the berg that he had just missed hitting by a yard or two nearly spoilt my supper of pasta and apple dumpling. We set a double watch—one man forward on lookout—until 2 a.m. when the fog cleared as the wind increased. There was far too much wind for the boomless mainsail which before breakfast, after a prolonged struggle, we got down. With so much belly in the sail we had to bring her into the wind before the throat halyards would render. Under the trys'l she still went at four knots, rolling with great abandon, so much so that Nicholas poured a jug of milk over me at breakfast.

Although we covered a lot of miles that day before this fresh quartering wind we did not outrun the bergs of which there were still far too many about. Curry and duff, for supper, by way of a change, encouraged me to dispense with a double watch for the oncoming night. There was a full moon and in the absence of fog I reckoned that bergs would show up from a mile or more away. However, coming on watch at 10 p.m. I soon realised that the moon was a hindrance rather than a help. Low in the sky and dead ahead, it turned the whole sea a silvery white, almost exactly the colour of ice. As a change from peering anxiously ahead I happened to glance aside where to my horror, barely three yards away, there was a piece of ice the size of a van with a long under-water tongue projecting towards us. We must have just skidded over it. As well as the moonlight, the breaking waves and the rise of the foredeck when the boat pitched, made it difficult to pick up anything directly ahead. The rest of my watch was spent literally and figuratively on tiptoe. On account of the over-high dog-house a short man always feels he is not seeing properly over it, and after this near-miss, having started breathing again, I felt in need of a hundred eyes and a powerful searchlight. A trawler that had passed us two nights before had kept his searchlight going all the time.

Further north in almost perpetual daylight icebergs are more a welcome break in a monotonous seascape than source of worry, but in the long nights of late summer further south, unless one is prepared to heave-to, they become something of a menace, for besides the berg itself there are the bergy bits and growlers to which they give birth and which are so much harder to spot. We were thankful when we saw what was to be our last, and two days later on 29th August we were well east of C. Farewell and a hundred miles to the south. For several days we had on board what bird-man Nicholas pronounced to be a dunlin. It soon got so used to us as to take food from our hands, any kind of food, not excluding curry and duff. For days on end the same gallant breeze blew steadily on our quarter, seldom more than force six and never less than force five, so that even without benefit of mainsail we made a fast passage. In thirty days from Holsteinborg to the Bishop light, sighted on 14th Sept., she averaged seventy miles a day, logging over a hundred miles on at least seven days. No homeward run can be too fast, especially when one has had, as it were, to retire hurt, and when there is a broken boom lying on deck to remind one of it.

We reached Lymington on 18th Sept. with twelve days in hand. Had we been assured of making so fast a passage home we might have gone on for another week, reaching possibly Upernavik (72° N.) but no further. That one can never be quite confident of reaching any of the places I aim at may be part of their charm, and failure is at least an excuse for making another voyage. Nevertheless, success is sweet and to achieve it in the case of Ellesmere Is. we ought to have started earlier, say mid-May, though even that would barely allow for unforeseen things like breaking booms. Travelling hopefully is within the reach of almost anyone while to arrive needs a little more judgment, determination, skill, and perhaps some luck. There are many ways to the top of a mountain but the view is always the same; and there are many ways of going to sea yet the views of those who do are various. Many go to compete, some for the excitement of speed, or for the thrills of passage-making, or merely to get away from it all. Some of us, by extending our horizons, are trying in an amateurish way to recapture or at least get a faint idea of days when, as Conrad wrote, 'the sea was great and mysterious and ready to surrender the prize of fame to audacious men.' Days most often of hardship and peril and never any lack of men to face them. To re-live their experiences may be impossible and to try to do so may be foolish but it was evidently the motive that inspired Hilaire Belloc's modest cruising, expressed in the words that I have already quoted: 'In venturing in sail upon strange coasts we are seeking those first experiences, and trying to feel as felt the earlier man in a happier time, to see the world as they saw it.'

PART THREE

East Greenland

1976

CHAPTER XII

A FALSE START

Lor, Brer Rabbit, you don' know what trouble is.
I'm de man what kin show you trouble.

UNCLE REMUS

As I BEGIN TO DESCRIBE THIS VOYAGE, the discrepancy between the target and the fall of shot provokes a wry smile. Wry smiles, I suppose, are better than no smiles but there will be few more of any kind. Only a Mark Tapley, who would take no credit for being jolly except in the most adverse conditions, only such a man could look with cheerful pleasure upon a voyage that thanks mainly to a half-hearted, dissident crew, missed its objective by a thousand miles and then failed with ignominy to bring the boat home.

Unlike the previous year, with winter merging into spring before I had had any offer, bite, or nibble from prospective crew, by Christmas I had gathered a promising nucleus. Owing to hard times the sail-training ship *Captain Scott*, based on the west coast of Scotland, had been laid up, and two of her former instructors, Brian Williamson and Hamish Brown, wrote to say they would like a voyage in *Baroque*. As well as their sea experience both were mountaineers. Then a man from Bristol offered to come. He had no sea experience so I suggested his coming as cook, to which he agreed with only moderate rapture. At the same time a David Burrows wrote to me about Spitzbergen. He was a retired business man (and a grandfather), owned a boat himself, and had had varied sailing experience including yacht deliveries. Living in Wells and keeping his boat in Wales he thus reversed my extraordinary habit of living in Wales and keeping a boat in Lymington. He wanted to sail his boat to Spitzbergen where she was to act as transport for a small shore-based expedition and having regard to the man and the boat this seemed to me a feasible plan. Later he wrote to say that nobody would insure the boat for Spitzbergen waters and instead offered to come with me to which I readily agreed. Since he had only a part share in the boat he could not afford to ignore the insurance aspect as I have had to do ever since I started sailing in 1954.

So there I was, long before sailing day, with a full crew, a crew that on paper, except for the Bristolian, abounded with promise. My state of euphoria can be imagined. Thus deeply committed there was no room for the faint-hearted doubts of the previous winter. Ellesmere Is.—for that must certainly be our aim—seemed almost in the bag. My monthly visits to *Baroque* at Lymington may have moderated this ardour but did not dispel it. There are few more depressing sights than the inside of a boat like *Baroque* on a wet, winter's day. In winter she has a great canvas tent rigged over the deck from stem to stern, and since this is tied down in about thirty places and the day is probably windy, I untie only enough to crawl under to go below. Naturally it is dark below though not too dark to discover that it is also damp. However, with the stove alight, a dry sleeping bag, and no watch on deck to keep, if it is not ecstasy it is comfort. All the same the cheerless surroundings became no brighter as I pondered over the defects that were being put right and the bills that would accrue. Primarily, of course, a new boom, solid this time. The doghouse windows had to be renewed and strengthened (a waste of time and money as it turned out); 10 ft. of underwater planking needed replacing; a samson post and the boom crutch were loose, as well as the engine seating. A soft spot in the mast needed an engraving piece which luckily could be done while the mast remained stepped. She had to be slipped for anti-fouling and for the repair of the planking, and finally a new lavatory had to be fitted, the old one having seized up solid. Altogether a thoroughly daunting amount of work to be done at present-day prices.

Of the crew so far I had met only David who called at Bodowen on the way to look at his boat lying in a small harbour a few miles north of Barmouth. The two Scots I took for granted, for surely with a background of climbing and sail training they would be of the right stuff; later Hamish looked me up on his way to the Atlas Mts. where he remained until a few days before we sailed. My Bristol man proved elusive. Twice I had advised him of my Lymington visits expecting that he would join me there to have a look at the boat, so that after his second failure to turn up I was not surprised to hear that he had taken another job and would not be available. I learnt this about a month before sailing day which I had fixed for 12th May, thus giving us three weeks start over that of 1975. On top of that came a letter from Brian Williamson to say that he had damaged a leg in a fall on Ben Nevis and would be out of action until the autumn. Thus at a stroke, as the politicians say, my crew had dwindled to two, one of whom, Hamish, would not be available for fitting out. Although this sort of thing had by now become usual I found it no less worrying.

But Brian Williamson was a responsible chap who appreciated my position and within a week had come up with the names of two Scottish climbers with whom I got in touch and who in the upshot made up the crew. Richard and Jim were bosom friends, both in their late twenties, married, and, I think, fathers, though that did not deter them from taking four months unpaid holiday. Nothing could be more outdated than two lines of Charles Kingsley:

> For men must work and women must weep,
> For there's little to earn and many to keep.

However, at that moment I was selfishly glad to have them and refrained from asking whether their wives had been consulted and what they thought. As Sancho remarked: 'A wife's counsel is bad, but he who will not take it is mad.' I did not see them until they joined though I learnt that Richard had had various jobs farming both in England and Norway, inshore fishing, and a spell as instructor at the Moray Firth Sea School. Two who joined us subsequently had also been there as instructors, so that even if this Sea School failed to furnish me with reliable hands it at least furnished a common topic of conversation and reminiscence. Jim, too, had had an unsettled career including a voyage as a refrigerator engineer. This distant connection with food impelled me to ask him to undertake the galley to which he willingly consented.

Thus thanks mainly to Brian Williamson we were again complete and I could proceed to Lymington in a fairly confident mood. David with his long experience would be a great asset; Hamish with his *Captain Scott* background should be more than useful; while Richard and Jim should at least be tough, for Scottish climbers, who do a lot of their climbing in winter, are reputedly hard men. During my absence Bodowen would be occupied at intervals by friends, or at least friends of a niece, for I myself for several obvious reasons have few friends left. It remained only to house in kennels my two dogs who can hardly have suspected a second act of treachery on master's part. That done I went down to Lymington on 1st May, the crew being due a day or two later. My first job was to set up the ratlines so that we could go aloft to start re-rigging the boat. Next day David arrived with a mountain of gear, a lot of it for the benefit of the ship—a bag of tools, an Aldis lamp, and a big quartz clock which kept remarkably accurate time, varying only a few seconds throughout the voyage. Richard and Jim came the following day, both burdened with more climbing equipment and gadgets than they were ever likely to use, especially on Ellesmere Is. where so far as I knew there were no peaks of Alpine character. Like yachting, climbing has been commercialised and those who participate are seemingly a 'soft sell' for the enterprising firms which provide superfluous but fashionable equipment. Richard appeared to be strong, well-built, fairly free from hair, while Jim, who was small, had hair down to his shoulders, reddish at that, not to mention a matted beard. He took pride in his hair, parting it in the middle and combing it admiringly in front of the small mirror in the galley. The beard's treatment was more offhand (the *mot juste*) merely being teasled out or scuffled with the fingers after meals to remove the bulkier debris. He had a powerful Scotch accent and later on, when his mouth became masked with hair, very few words that I could understand ever filtered through.

With Hamish still to come the four of us had enough to do to be ready in time. David at once showed his quality by taking on the manifold jobs that required some technical knowledge and skill with tools. Enthusiasm was rife as it always is either when fitting out for a long voyage, at the start of a mountaineering expedition, or even at the start of a war. A mountain expedition is usually short enough for enthusiasm to be sustained right up to the end. Wars may last for years but even for voyages that are reckoned in months enthusiasm at the start is not enough. More solid and less effervescent qualities are needed such as determination, endurance, forbearance, a sense of duty, and an obligation towards the ship we serve. Sir Francis Drake, that sovereign leader of men, may have had in mind this all too likely fading of early enthusiasm: 'It is not the beginning,' as he said, 'but the continuing of the same until it be thoroughly finished that yieldeth the true glory.'

On 10th May we embarked the stores. The lack of dried egg, apparently unobtainable, was a nuisance. Although duffs can be and were made by Jim without they are all the better when eggs are included; and in the form of scrambled egg or omelette, provided it is well laced with Tabasco sauce, dried egg makes a welcome change from porridge for breakfast. Everything that was not in tins had to be packed in plastic bags. On land one curses the plastic in which everything from wood screws to kippers is nowadays impenetrably wrapped, yet what a blessing it is to the man in a small boat, especially to one whose boat is inclined to be wet, either for protecting his bunk, his clothes, or his food. In the Himalaya before the plastic age had dawned one had to have bags made specially from canvas or some rubberised material for carrying the loads of sugar, atta, or satu, if they were to survive the monsoon rains or the mishaps that occur when fording rivers.

Hamish arrived that day and from the lack of interest he bestowed on our activities one had the impression that he rather regretted having left the Atlas Mts. Enthusiasm, whether to be sustained or not, was noticeably lacking. Certainly he had been travelling hard since leaving the Atlas, including a journey to Scotland, and possibly the contrast between *Captain Scott* and *Baroque* took some digesting. From April onwards the weather had been good with a lot of easterly winds, perfect conditions for a swift and painless passage down Channel, allowing the crew time to find their sea-legs. It broke just before we sailed—rain, westerlies, and gale warnings all round the coast. We had other worries, too, in the form of an intrusion by Southern Television who threatened to come again to see us off in spite of all the discouragement I could give them. Television camera men think they are conferring a favour by allowing you to appear in some obscure programme along with other unfortunates as obscure as oneself; whereas for thus making you look and feel a fool some compensation is surely due from them, preferably in kind—a coil of rope or a bottle of whisky.

Still having some mistrust of *Baroque*'s steering when under power I arranged for a tow through the narrowest part of the channel—expensive yachts lying on either hand—to as far as the fuelling berth where we had to fill up with diesel oil. The fact that it was raining and blowing hard did not prevent the camera men from carrying out their threat at a time when we had much to do besides mouthing vocables into a microphone while striking seamanlike attitudes. One of our fuel tanks had moved, as we belatedly discovered, making it extremely awkward to fill; and the twice-baked bread delivered the previous evening needed supplementing. There had to be enough of this to see us to Greenland and instead of twenty-four large loaves they had sent small loaves. An old and tried friend who was on board dashed off to the town, the shops not yet open, where by some undisclosed means he obtained a quantity of biscuit—the more or less edible cardboard variety. At nine o'clock we cast off and started down the river under our own steam, the Royal Lymington Yacht Club honouring us with a two-gun salute as we passed their clubhouse. *Baroque* played no tricks and although I am just wise enough to insure against third-party risks while in home waters, upon our reaching the river mouth clear of the lines of moored yachts I heave a sigh of relief. We were by no means there yet, but even more profound is the relief felt when clear of the British Isles. As Conrad wrote: 'The true peace of God begins a thousand miles from the nearest land.'

Arrived in the Solent, in view of the strong westerly wind, we decided to anchor to await better times as we have had to do on several previous occasions. There is something to be said for starting on the appointed day even if it does mean anchoring outside. The last minute shopping for forgotten items which threatens to go on and on is finally halted, those few who have come to see one off are not disappointed, while the crew, most of them with scant resources, can buy no more beer. By morning the wind had veered north-west and the barometer had risen so that in spite of the early shipping forecast which still muttered gale warnings we got under way with all plain sail, able to lay the course for the Needles channel. For the benefit of my friend Mr. Lee, who had got us our biscuit and who, as I expected, was now lurking there in wait with his camera, we went as close as we could to Hurst Point. Outside the Needles where the wind had free play we put a roll in the mains'l and dropped the stays'l. The evening forecast spoke of south-west winds of force seven to eight whereas the wind fell light with none at all at times. Hamish seemed seedy but the rest shaped well.

No favouring slant of wind came our way. Contrary winds pushed us into Lyme Bay and early on the 16th, the same W.S.W. wind blowing and a gale warning for the Plymouth area, I decided to anchor inside Start Point. The poor progress we were making hardly justified the effort and a calm spell might give Hamish, who now looked the worse for wear, a better chance of recovery. He had eaten nothing beyond some dates from the Atlas Mts. and except for standing his watch had remained prone ever since the start. He had unwisely told us that *Captain Scott* had been accustomed to leaving harbour when other vessels were seeking shelter and we could not help wondering how he had managed on those occasions. All next day we remained at anchor. To give our table a much needed new look David planed and holystoned it, while Richard and Jim went ashore for bread and a jerrycan of water. Having got doused in the surf they brought back some mouldy rolls wrapped in plastic, so this foray was not a success and one hoped that no eagle-eyed coast watcher had noted it and reported back to the Lymington Customs.

Out at sea again we raised the Eddystone light that night and by the 20th, a rough, windy day, when we were a week out from Lymington, we were still the wrong side of the Lizard. The crew were not cheerful and the presence of the melancholy Hamish holding his head in his hands did nothing to raise their spirits. The next day, as for some time I had expected and feared, he expressed a wish to be put ashore and in spite of the delay and doubt about finding a replacement I thought it best to comply. Luckily we were not too far off and the wind was fair for Falmouth. This was where I had bought *Baroque* in 1972 and mindful of the trouble I have had with her and was yet to have I sometimes wonder why. Was she a replica of Milton's 'fatal and perfidious bark, built in th' eclipse and rigged with curses dark'? Or was her skipper at fault, trying too high a faithful old servant, subjecting her to Chinese gybes, strandings, and the shunting of ice? As we made fast to a convenient buoy that evening the Customs launch came alongside. They sealed up our bonded stores and in reply to enquiries told us that our convenient buoy might cost us £1.50 a day. Though on pleasure bent, like Mrs. Gilpin, I have a frugal mind so we moved forthwith to an anchorage. That done I went ashore to the Royal Cornwall Y.C. to make my number and to ask for the use of their telephone. That was all I expected and in fact all I got, for I knew it would be no use enquiring there for crew. Later Richard and Jim put in calls to Manchester and Fort William thus making our shortage known in their respective circles. Hamish, now restored to health, left next day. Having contributed nothing to the gaiety of nations while at sea he now made amends by capsizing the dinghy alongside and falling into the drink. For the first and last time on the voyage the crew enjoyed a wholehearted laugh. Hamish then got away in a motor boat (owned by yet another Moray Sea School Old Boy) wringing out his clothes as he went. This was on a Saturday and Jim had already hoisted in what that implied—curry and duff for supper.

On the Sunday, with an easterly wind blowing powerfully enough to have set us on our way a hundred miles or more, I landed on the Flushing shore and walked across to Mylor where *Baroque* had been fitted out for her first voyage. At the boatyard there I met the manager and a shipwright I knew who, as I had hoped, had someone for me in mind and strongly recommended him. After some search we learnt that he was away on a delivery job. At Flushing on the way back a young chap accosted me and having had a look at *Baroque* professed interest in the voyage. He had a job with a local tin-mining company and after dithering over the week-end finally decided in favour of tin. On the Monday I had another nibble from a curious chap who had neither house, flat, nor caravan but dwelt snail-like in his Volkswagen. He, too, was a yacht delivery man working for an agent in Plymouth. He would consult his agent, he said, and telephone me Yes or No at 10.30 a.m. the next day. No call came and I suppose it was idle to expect promises to be kept by a man whose home was in a motor car. Having waited until 11 a.m. I was about to push off in the dinghy when the club steward ran out to say there was a call for me. The steward of the Royal Cornwall, by the way, proved more helpful than the members. Evidently the jungle drums had been rumbling to some purpose, from the Scottish highlands to the south of England. A Mike Holland, speaking from Chichester, knew all about us and our need, seemed bent on joining, but thought it might take him a week to get ready. I suggested he should come down and have a look at me and the boat. He arrived that evening all kitted up and wanting only a morning in Falmouth for a final round-up. He slept on board while mother, who had driven him down, parked herself in a hotel. Mike, too, had been an instructor at the Moray Sea School, and although not a dedicated worker was a good hand and a likeable chap. Unluckily he proved to be ill adapted for a long voyage.

CHAPTER XIII

THE TURNING POINT

W E SAILED ON THE 26TH, a fortnight having already elapsed since we left Lymington, the crew change costing us nearly a week. It could have been much longer. Anchored in the roads were two smart French brigantines, sail training ships presumably, with two yards on the foremast, fore and aft rig on the main. Richard the fishing expert got to work and late that evening off the Lizard had a good haul of mackerel which we had for breakfast fried in oatmeal. And à propos of fishing, we witnessed an amusing scene near the Wolf rock the next afternoon—two French fishing boats speeding southwards, bursting their boilers, so to speak, the reason for their haste becoming clear when a naval vessel hove in sight well astern of them. At the time, and it was a rare event, we had our genoa set, a huge sail hanked to the topmast forestay imposing a severe strain on the mast. That would have been acceptable had there been any topmast backstays but after the first voyage I had abolished these in order to simplify the gear and cut out chafe, the genoa being so rarely set. One had to watch the topmast and guess how much it would bend before worse happened. When we had this sail up again next day we soon had to take it down on account of a heavy swell which made the mast whip. Unlike *Mischief* and *Sea Breeze*, both fitted with fidded topmasts that could be sent down, *Baroque* has a pole mast. To have the mast cut short, though it would suit my purposes, would certainly spoil her graceful appearance. She had no tops'l when I bought her and I have not had one made. Such a sail might be of value in Greenland waters where in summer light winds are the rule rather than the exception, and the reeving of the extra gear could be delayed until one had got there.

To come to a more homely subject, after this nautical digression. Originally in the 'heads' compartment there had been a shower as well as the lavatory. If you were shower-minded you stood in a deep well, the feet no doubt in bilge water; but we had always used the well for

155

stowing bonded stores. The bulkheads surrounding this insanitary affair were lined with bits of black imitation stone, like sequins, the whole effect one of sombre gloom. David took this in hand. Abolished the taps and pipes (from which, rather surprisingly, water spurted), stripped the bulkheads and painted them white, boarded over the bottomless well, fitted shelves above, provided a footstool for the lavatory seat, and for good measure a handhold for use in rough weather. To commemorate this welcome transformation Richard affixed a plaque:

> This loo designed and built
> By David Burrows
> Shipwright 1976

An obvious mistake in the spelling of 'shipwright' had to be put right. Spurred on by this the crew had one of their infrequent attacks of spontaneous effort. The brass lamps were polished and the panelling in the cabin—mahogany, I believe—given a shine. Of the gimballed brass lamps that look so well few survive the voyage; the brass fittings corrode and the globes break. As a general routine David worked most of the day, either on the engine, or tracking down leaks and stopping them, or many small jobs that were of benefit to the ship; Richard and Jim read voraciously or held long private conferences, while Mike mostly slept.

Meantime we had rounded the Seven Stones and were making some progress. Richard caught five unusually large mackerel and, as often happens, several racing pigeons alighted on board. The one to which we entrusted our message to mankind refused to push off until it had Ireland in sight. South of the Fastnet we had some roughish weather which laid Jim out and we had to forego our Saturday night curry and duff. The winds were mostly from the wrong direction and in the first week out from Falmouth we had made good a pitiful 240 miles. In the second week we did better, logging just under 400 miles, for by then we were beyond the influence of the anti-cyclonic weather that prevailed over the British Isles for most of a memorable summer. Iceland, on the other hand, had a very poor summer, while in the North Atlantic the month of June which is usually fairly quiet proved to be pretty boisterous. Besides a frightening bang like that from a 15-inch gun as Concorde passed overhead there were other disconcerting incidents. Because I had the mains'l down for stitching, we were motoring when Jim discovered that the port side fuel tank had again shifted and was dripping oil on to the hot exhaust pipe. The tank had to be emptied before we could get it upright and secured for a full due. A moderate gale on the 8th June broke a pane in the galley skylight and an immoderate gale the following night made her leak so much that we handed the sails and lay-a-hull. The drips from the deck-head over my bunk obliged me to rig plastic gutters under two of the beams; but strangely enough Richard's bunk, almost directly under the fore-hatch, remained driest of all.

A flat calm on the 10th induced us to make use of the engine when we discovered the batteries were flat. Jim attributed this to salt water though in the doghouse where the batteries live there had so far been nothing more serious than drips. David immediately set about converting the anchor winch handle into a starting handle, and at that time there may have been just enough left in the batteries for this plan to succeed. Meantime with no engine and no compass light we were still a lot better off than earlier Greenland-bound voyagers. 'Hellish dark and smells of cheese,' was James Pigg's report on the night's weather, having when drunk looked into a cupboard instead of out of a window. So it was that night except for the smell, and the darkness was accentuated by a featureless layer of cloud that blended sea and sky together indistinguishably. Without a compass steering was difficult and within five minutes of taking over from me David executed a Chinese gybe, so I went back and stayed on until it began to get light. In such conditions one needs to discard hoods, hats, and towels round the neck in order to steer by feeling the wind.

Saturday 12th June might be called Black Saturday in that it put paid to any hope of our reaching Ellesmere Is. After heavy squalls of wind and rain the previous evening the sky had cleared but the wind remained fresh. With three rolls in the mains'l we were heading north, the best we could do, and at the awkward hour of 5 a.m. a seam in the mains'l started to go. By the time enough hands had mustered to get the sail down some twenty feet of seam had gone as well as some bad tears crosswise. This was a serious blow for I could see little chance of repairing the sail at sea. It is far too big to have below for stitching and this could be done on deck only in more or less windless weather.

These horizontal seams were a nuisance. A tear of an inch or so soon became an ell, and after the last voyage I had made a mental note to have narrow strips sewn every few feet vertically from head to foot. For me mental notes are not enough with the result that nothing had been done. On this occasion, after the sail had been repaired in rather amateurish fashion by a Reykjavik sailmaker, I added some cross strips myself. On land, bolting the stable door after the horse's departure is a well-known exercise; at sea it takes the form of handing a sail after it is ripped. With the wind backing and the glass falling, as they were, prudence should have suggested setting the trys'l instead of reefing the mains'l. The trouble is that roller reefing is too easy so that instead of changing sails one is inclined merely to put in more rolls.

This was only the start of Black Saturday. We set the trys'l, and after breakfast it began to blow in earnest, the barometer having fallen to 992 mbs. At two o'clock when we were doing five knots and making a lot of water, not to mention the odd spout through the skylight, we handed the trys'l and pressed on under the jib. Two hours later this had to come down for the sea had built up and waves were beginning to break with the usual menacing roars. Lying-a-hull with no sails set the vessel lies broadside on to wind and sea. Whether this is better or worse than heaving-to, when with a minimum of sail set she takes wind and sea on the weather bow, is a moot point. In either case the drift to leeward is the same, from twenty to thirty miles a day in a full gale. If lying-a-hull, there are no sails to blow out and there may be less strain on the rudder, on the other hand, if broadside on, a boat is more vulnerable than when lying bow on, especially if like *Baroque* she has a lofty and fragile doghouse. We had not been lying-a-hull long before a wave broke alongside and bashed in the starboard side of this erection, flooding the chartroom (for that is what is inside) with all the charts, navigational books, log books, sextant, chronometer watch, not to mention the batteries which on this occasion really did have a salt water bath. David got to work boarding up the hole and for good measure put boards over the port side as well. Meantime I got her before the wind and we ran under bare poles, a stratagem that did not escape the notice of Poseidon, ruler of the waves, for one of these promptly broke over the counter, cracking a bit more of the doghouse, filling the cockpit, and in its retreat nearly dragging the skipper through the life-rails.

To keep her before the wind with no sail set was not easy and when darkness fell we once more lay-a-hull. It blew hard until morning when the wind veered north-west and dropped to a steady force six at which it remained all day. Richard retired from his watch at 2 a.m. to remain all day in his bunk suffering as he said from 'exposure'. Except for David, the crew seemed to be a little shaken by this gale. As I surveyed the scene on deck Mike took me aback by remarking that he assumed we should now be returning home, and no doubt he was equally astonished by my reply. He then said he would quit at the first opportunity and all three were decided we should go to Reykjavik for repairs, then about 500 miles to the north. Cape Farewell, for which the wind might be less favourable, was about 600 and from there to Godthaab another 400 miles. The lack of mains'l and engine, and the impossibility of finding at Godthaab a replacement for Mike, inclined me at first to agree; though over-riding these arguments should have been the fact that going to Reykjavik implied giving up Ellesmere Is. My own private thoughts about Mike were that if we got to Godthaab, the fact that we were still afloat and the high cost of getting away from there as compared with Reykjavik, might induce him to change his mind.

For the next three days the weather continued boisterous, though with winds mainly from west we were able to lay the course for Iceland. The serving of the eye-splice of the forestay round the mast had come off and to my annoyance chafed through the jib halyard, an almost new terylene rope. With no jib our speed fell off dismally and several days elapsed before we could get Jim aloft in his climbing harness with a top rope to reeve a new halyard. David made and discarded several versions of a starting handle for the engine and when his Mark V version, from which he expected success, failed like the others, he gave it up as a bad job.

The wind then began blowing from the direction of Iceland right in our teeth and when this had gone on for two days I altered course for C. Farewell hoping that by now the others would have recovered their nerve and see reason. We were then on the same latitude about 500 miles away and the wind was fair. Jim, who had become spokesman for the malcontents at once protested, calling it an 'undemocratic' decision, and at the sailor's Soviet he presently convened David and I found ourselves in a minority. Had I had any eloquence now was the time for an appeal to their better natures or even to their self-respect, but I felt mere disgust and no doubt allowed it to show. For me the voyage had now no aim and I could not feel much regard for those who had so tamely abandoned its objective. They were not the ill-conditioned lot that I had suffered from in '68 on *Mischief*'s last southern voyage—I felt no likelihood of being pushed overboard or knocked on the head— they merely lacked the requisite zeal. Giving up Ellesmere Is. also meant my failing to keep a promise of calling at Igdlorssuit, where we had been on *Baroque*'s first voyage, in order to bring back a Zodiac left there by a friend of mine, Professor Drever, who had recently died. To press on with an unwilling crew, who apparently expected the next gale to sink us, would be an ill task for which I had neither will nor strength. It is easy to criticise. When reviling it is not necessary to prepare a pre- liminary draft, but it occurs to me that for the state of affairs we had then reached I should have reviled myself. In the army one learnt that there were no bad regiments, battalions, batteries, there were only bad officers, and in the present case the skipper who had recruited his crew in the first place and who then failed to jolly them along and to infect them with some notion of high endeavour, was himself to blame. That said there is the truism about silk purses and sow's ears, and the fact that you can't hang soft cheese on iron hooks.

So once more we headed north, or rather well west of north which was the best we could point. And since the north-easterly wind contin- ued to blow, in four days time we were in the latitude of Reykjavik and 120 miles west of it. Had we stood on for C. Farewell we should have rounded it by then. Angmagssalik on the east coast of Greenland was almost as near as Reykjavik. David suggested our going there, ignor- ing or ignorant of the fact that at this time of year, late June, ice con- ditions would almost certainly prevent it. Waiting in vain for a shift of wind we stayed too long on the starboard tack and by the time we went about to steer south-east we were nearly 150 miles north-west of our destination. At midnight of the 24th the wind, still at north-east, increased to gale force and although this gale had less vice than the earlier one the damage it did was more serious.

Under trys'l and jib she was going fast and working too much. In order to heave-to we had to drop the jib and set the reefed stays'l, and no sooner had the jib been dropped and the support given by its tight luff wire withdrawn, than the forestay parted. This three-inch circum-ference wire, in apparently good shape, passes inside the stemhead for almost a foot before emerging at deck level. The unseen bit inside the stemhead had rusted and there it parted. This in turn endangered the mast. In the lower part of the mast there is a long scarph which then began opening and shutting in ominous fashion as the mast swayed. Having downed the trys'l we managed to set up the forestay temporar-ily by means of a wire strop round the bowsprit and a tackle; and in daylight I managed to get the stay really tight with a length of chain rove through the stemhead and back to the anchor winch. It was too rough to deal with the mast. We did this next day when David and I put three wide bands of fencing wire round it. That done we set both jib and trys'l and crossed our fingers.

A fortnight had now passed since we turned north for Iceland. After copious priming with boiling water and a blow lamp heating the air-intake David made one more attempt to start the engine. By now, of course, not a flicker of life remained in the batteries. No joy, there-fore, except that David lost his cool with the crew who were being less than helpful. The 28th, gloomy and cold, saw the last of our twice-baked bread and we turned to our edible cardboard. That night when the wind rose to nearly gale force we handed all sails, having in mind the state of the mast, a state that Mr. Chucks the bosun might have described as precarious and not very permanent. As we rolled and tossed, with no sails to steady her, a trawler passed, the first vessel we had seen for several weeks. Richard wished he was on board. On the contrary, I thought, they had reason to envy us who had nothing to do but lie and read in our lamp-lit bunks, in cool and airy surround-ings instead of hot and stuffy, with no engine thumping away, and no racing propeller as she pitched.

Our mishaps were by no means over. We were aiming for Garhskali, a low, rocky point on the southern side of the wide Faxafloi bight at the back of which lies Reykjavik. On 30th June, when we had run our dis-tance eastwards, confirmed by a snap sight which I got between rain squalls, Mike spotted an isolated rock of a peculiar shape. There was no such rock anywhere near Garhskali and by a process of elimination and comparison with views in the *Arctic Pilot* we decided it must be Eldey nearly twenty miles south of Garhskali. Eldey is a sheer-sided rock about

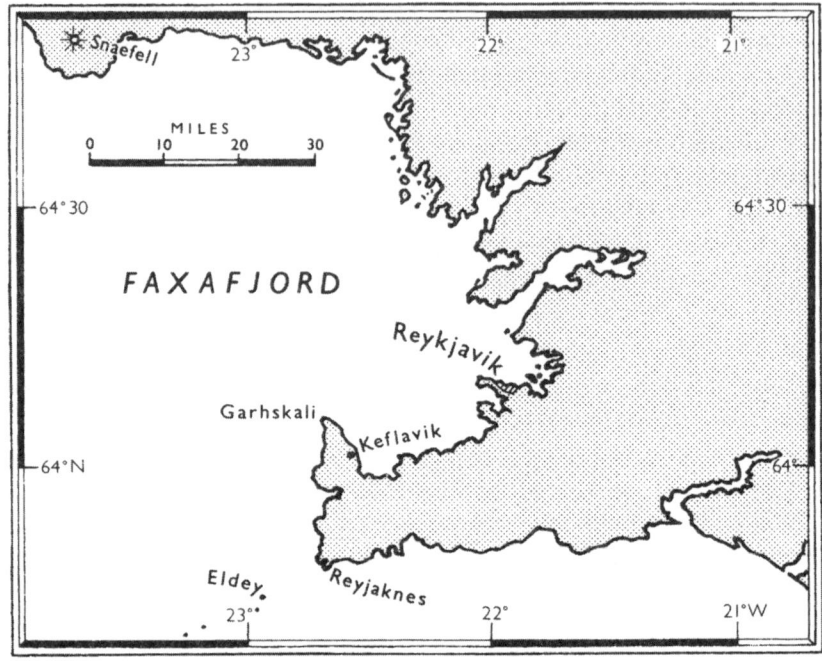

Map 4: Approaches to Reykjavik

220 ft. high lying off the coast about eight miles south-west of Reyjaknes at the south-west corner of the mainland. Until recently it was one of the largest gannetries in the world. Now the gannets seem to have been ousted by fulmars. It is unlit and from it a dangerous reef extends for thirty miles to the south-west. Had we not sighted Eldey we should have missed Iceland altogether and gone bumming on to the south-east. On this occasion the navigator was not entirely at fault, though he might have discovered earlier that the compass had resumed its behaviour of the previous voyage. Instead of the four points westerly variation that in this region it should have shown it had less than one point; so that when we were steering southeast by compass on the assumption that that would be east true, we were in fact steering nearly south-east true.

We closed the rock and having sighted Reyjaknes and its lighthouse, thus confirming that the rock was Eldey, we rounded it and made north up the coast. The wind had at last gone round to west putting us on a lee shore, a shore that remained obstinately hidden under low cloud throughout the day. Intent on keeping a good offing we steered west of north with the result that when we had run our distance to Garhskali we were a long way from the coast. We raised the Garhskali light that night and in the morning (1st July) a light breeze took us into Reykjavik roadstead where we anchored close to the harbour entrance. At the worst we could take a battery ashore for charging in order to use the engine for entering the harbour. However, when I went ashore to see the Customs and the harbourmaster the latter at once agreed to tow us in. A pilot came off that afternoon and as he watched patiently while we laboriously wound in the anchor cable with a Stilson wrench I wondered what he thought of us. The winch handle with which David had hoped to start the engine had not yet been restored to its original condition. We secured alongside a big floating crane, a convenient berth just abaft of five Icelandic gunboats, the whole fleet. They were dressed over-all in honour of the fifitieth anniversary of the Coastguard service and most of them were still undergoing repairs to hull damage sustained in the recent cod-war. Any ideas we may have had that the Red Ensign would not be welcome in Reykjavik were soon to be dismissed. We needed help of various kinds and willing helpers were easily found. The Icelanders no doubt felt they had been victorious and perhaps on that account were all the more ready to be generous to the defeated.

CHAPTER XIV

FROM REYKJAVIK TO ANGMAGSSALIK

WHEN WE PUT IN HERE in 1972 to have a new boom made for *Sea Breeze* the local Odin Yacht Club had found for us the right man for the job. Through the Customs I tried to get in touch with them again. Nothing happened and no one from the Yacht Club ever came near us; instead the man himself, Jon Jonason, who had made the boom, turned up next morning accompanied by one Stefan Bjarnason as interpreter. Stefan deserves a word to himself for he became our main standby, sparing neither time nor trouble on our behalf. He was a naval architect by profession having studied at Newcastle University. After a spell in Nyasaland working for U.N.O. designing fishing boats for use on Lake Nyasa, he had returned to Reykjavik where he now had the job of Harbour Pollution Inspector. Like many others in Reykjavik, where inflation is probably worse than in England, he had to have two jobs to make ends meet; after office hours, which were not unduly prolonged, he worked in his own profession.

Jon Jonason, widely known in Reykjavik as Jon Eleven (he had in his time been a noted footballer), has a small boat-building yard where he employs himself, his son, and one other hand. He has a liking for old boats and loves working in wood; in his shed was the hull of a 60 ft. fishing boat which he expected to finish by the end of the year. In Iceland fishing boats have to be built to a very high standard and this one looked enormously strong. In his spare time Jon had built himself a small yacht—sails, fittings, and engine bought from England, the latter, I regret to say, proving highly unsatisfactory. Later on he sailed her round from his yard five miles away to bring up alongside us at our floating crane. To Jon I entrusted the job of repairing and strengthening the doghouse and of making up three iron bands for the mast. Having taken our batteries away for recharging he started work the same afternoon. Stefan took me to a wholesale fishmonger where I bought a kilogramme of halibut for £1.50. There are no fishmonger shops in Reykjavik (nor any butchers); presumably most of the 70,000 people living there get their fish from relatives or friends employed in fishing or in fish factories. Later when we moved to that side of the harbour where the fishing boats lie we were given all the fish we needed. Stefan presented me with some dried cod, stockfish, which is eaten raw like chewing gum, only worse. It is very expensive.

Before he left home Mike and the two other climbers were to spend a week in the mountains a long bus journey north of Reykjavik. Richard and Jim, by now practically penniless, had no qualms about allowing Mike to foot the bill, for nowadays the young expect and accept hand-outs from the Government milch-cow or from individuals as of right. Thus David and I had some time alone on board, a pleasant respite. On Sundays we used to walk out to the Meteorological Office, now housed in a new building some way beyond the airport. They had copies of the most recent ice charts from the Met. Office at Bracknell and now that our dwindling ambitions comprised only a brief visit to Angmagssalik we were interested in the ice conditions off the east coast. These appeared to be bad, or at least worse than normal, and were not likely to improve before the end of July or early August. We had a look, too, at the North Atlantic weather chart for 12th and 13th June which showed a large depression covering our position at that time with a low at the centre of 975 mbs. Those on duty there on Sundays welcomed our intrusion and gave us all the information they could, usually in perfect English. To get inside I found embarrassing, for the main door was kept locked and one had to press a button and speak into a hole in the wall to explain who one was. Usually a girl's voice replied in dulcet but distorted tone. I felt like Pyramus conversing with Thisbe: 'O sweet, O lovely wall, thanks courteous wall.'

One day a French yacht with a cheerful and capable crew of three came alongside, two months out via the Hebrides and the Faroes. They knew all about *Mischief*'s voyages and were the first yachtsmen I have met who had similar aims, indeed even larger aims. On a voyage of indefinite extent they intended visiting the west coast of Greenland, Baffin Is., Labrador, California, Alaska, and thence down to the Patagonia channels, in fact most of the cold, mountainous regions that could be reached by sea. They had not quite done their homework, for they were not aware that they would probably meet ice off south-west

Greenland, their first objective. I advised them to make for Godthaab and the mountains to the north and gave them my west Greenland charts of which they had very few. It would have done my three faint-hearted voyagers a world of good to have met these French lads and to have caught some of their bold, infectious spirit.

Meantime *Baroque* needed attention, primarily the forestay both below and aloft where the eye-splice had to be parcelled and served. The jib halyard rove by Jim had also been stranded. I only discovered this when sitting aloft in the bosun's chair serving the splice suspended on that same halyard, or rather by the one frayed strand that remained. To replace the chain at deck level I got from a kindly stevedore a discarded two-and-a-half-inch wire sling, cut off the damaged bit, and put a hard eye in one end. An equally kind engineering shop made up a long threaded 'U' bolt which served for tightening up instead of an expensive bottle screw. The other end of the sling was secured to the broken forestay with bulldog grips and to disguise this I covered the whole with overhand grafting painted black, decorated with Turk's Heads painted white. Besides the forestay both wire topping lifts needed attention, one having to be replaced with rope. Of necessity the mast bands that Jon Eleven fitted had large outstanding lugs to take the bolts. As these hindered sail hoisting David made wood fairings to fit above and below the lugs so that the sail lacing would render over them. This worked pretty well although both the mains'l and trys'l lacing sometimes needed assisting over them by hand.

On 13th July the climbing party returned refreshed by the change of scene; Richard, for a time, slightly less bloody-minded. Mike left next day with assurances that he would send out a substitute. We had had one or two nibbles from Icelanders and from the Youth Hostel where we had made our want known. There was probably no connection but on the return of the climbing party I suffered a sleepless night. Consequently in the afternoon, having finished *The Times* crossword, I was dozing off when one of the pilots came on board to move us in order to make room for *Brendan*. This was the boat made from thirty-two cow-hides on a voyage from Ireland to America. Better off in one respect than St. Brendan she had made her whereabouts known by radio telephone and she had also been sighted some eighty miles away. Rather than secure outside us, as she could have done, she was to have

VIP treatment, and in view of the numbers of sight-seers who would want to go on board her we did well to be out of it. Owing to adverse winds three more days elapsed before *Brendan* arrived to receive a great welcome. To give her a fresh coating of some special grease they later slipped the boat at a yard near Jon's place where David and I had a look at her. They told us she was an excellent sea-boat and could do wonders with a following wind having on occasions logged over 100 miles a day on passage from the Faeroes. There was some talk of crew changes but I had no fear of any of my crew volunteering for the next leg of this bold and remarkably uncomfortable adventure. But on our return to Reykjavik later we learnt that she never sailed, a long spell of westerly winds having decided the crew to leave her there for the winter. Would St. Brendan have concurred?

Our move across the harbour did not go smoothly. Besides cutting with its propeller the moorings of a small boat, the pilot boat that had us in tow rammed the quay wall with our bowsprit. On reaching the other side we were put in a berth alongside a wooden quay that at high tide would be submerged. A fishing boat owner suggested our lying against a nearby trawler that was undergoing repair and offered to tow us there. He did this with so much elan that our counter hit the steel hull of the trawler a terrible crack, starting a plank and displacing the counter itself a good three inches. More work for Jon Eleven's shipwright who next day made good the plank and restored and strengthened the counter.

When the mains'l came back repaired we bent it on, Richard assisting, after which he announced his forthcoming departure, his passage home already arranged for with the British Consul. I made some suitable remark upon which he went below in dudgeon to confer with Jim who by now seemed to be the senior in this strange partnership. A few minutes later he was back on deck with the news that he had now decided to stay to which I foolishly consented. From the Consul, whom I knew of old, I learnt that he had merely outlined to Richard the necessary procedure when applying for assistance as a distressed British subject; among other things he would have had to produce a note from me saying that I refused to take him. A surprising number of people had been assisted back from Iceland in the past year and, less surprisingly, many of them had failed to refund the money. The same day I had a too laconic cable from Mike—'Crew arriving 23rd'—which aroused speculation as to who this crew might be. In order of dread I feared it might be either a friend of Richard's, the girl with whom Mike had sailed home from the West Indies, an instructor from the Moray Sea School, or even Mike himself, by this time possibly regretting that he had not kept his hand to the plough. Richard now did his best to behave normally, even doing some work, instead of remaining aloof surrounded by an aura of morose gloom, or what may have been merely the mystic melancholy of a Scot too far from home; an attitude that in the army as I first knew it would have quickly had him booked by the sergeant-major on a charge of dumb insolence.

Varying our route, David and I walked one Sunday to the Met. Office by way of the beach where we came across a stream of hot water gushing out of a large drainpipe. This was a popular picnic spot where numerous families in bathing dresses larked about in the hot stream. All the houses and buildings in Reykjavik are heated by this constant supply of hot water from underground. Stefan showed us his modest bills for so many tons of hot water; at his house there were two inlets, one for the radiators and one for the hot taps. His water when used went down the drain but in newer houses the supply is re-cycled. Thus there is some compensation for living on an unstable island with the ever-present threat of eruptions.

The latest ice chart showed little change for the better and there were reports of a vessel having been stuck in the ice for two weeks. On the other hand, a pilot who had just flown back from Kulusuk, the air-strip 16 miles E.N.E. of Angmagssalik, told me that the ice looked navigable; but what might look navigable from a thousand feet up might not look so good from *Baroque*'s cross-trees. Hoping for some real information from a man on the spot I went to the Danish consul and got the telephone number of Niels Underborg, skipper of a boat based at Angmagssalik, who had been of assistance to me in the past. No reply could be got from this Angmagssalik number (which saved me a costly telephone call) and later I found that Niels had retired to Denmark. For some odd reason the use of a telephone to obtain information about ice conditions seemed to me a little underhand. The early seamen-explorers, whose experience it has always been my aim in a faint and feeble way to recapture, had to go and find out; and in

We were made welcome in Reykjavik,
with a berth near some Icelandic gunboats

spite of ice reports, which are out of date by the time one is on the spot, this is what the man in a small boat has nowadays still to do. Anyway, our new crew having arrived as promised on the 23rd. I decided to sail on the 29th, hoping that by the time we were off the coast in early August the ice would be navigable. The new crew, another Hamish, a big chap and a climber, who was from the Moray Sea School, proved also, like Mike, to lack staying power. With a crew that in words of studious moderation might be called mercurial it is a mistake to visit such unremote places as Reykjavik or Angmagssalik from which escape is comparatively easy.

At considerable cost we stocked up with bread, rice, fish-loaf, potatoes, and onions, taking only enough for a month as I reckoned food would be cheaper in Angmagssalik assuming we got there. Shortly before we sailed a small vessel belonging to the Danish Geodetic Survey came in with eight geologists on board bound for East Greenland. She was named *Tycho Brahe* after the Danish astronomer and later she was to do me what I considered an ill turn. On the day we sailed, a day of incessant rain, Jon Eleven came to say farewell with a gift of two boxes of frozen haddock fillets earmarked for the American market, in other words the best. We cast off after lunch, but before we had cleared Engey Island not far from the harbour entrance, finding the wind dead ahead and the weather thick, we turned back and anchored in the roadstead. We beat out next day in better weather and when off Gardhskagi we hove-to in the hope of catching some cod. Richard had provided himself with lures recommended by the professionals but we had no luck; what with the tide and the boat fore-reaching, as she does when hove-to, we were probably moving too much.

In crossing Denmark Strait we had a lot of rain and winds of such variable strength that we spent most of the time reefing and unreefing. It is about 400 miles across and on 14th August, when we were less than a hundred miles from the Greenland coast the sea temperature dropped from 9°C. at 6 a.m. to 3°C. at noon, indicating that we were then in the East Greenland current. At 3 a.m. next day when we were bowling along before a nice easterly breeze, the weather was so thick that I decided to double the watch with one man on look-out. So on being relieved at the helm I went forward and, as I had expected, soon began to sight the odd ice floe. By breakfast time we were surrounded by scattered floes and having retreated to open water we steered north-west along the edge of what I thought must be a detached field of ice—at least one hoped it was for we were still a long way from the coast. The previous evening Jim had reported hearing a distant rumble, a noise that no doubt came from this field of ice. A noon sight put us about fifty-five miles E.S.E. of C. Dan and by evening we were some thirty miles from the land with ice visible ahead as well as to north and south. The glass was falling so we retreated a few miles to the west and hove-to.

This prudent decision failed to save us from a night of anxiety. When I took over at midnight from David he stayed up, for what with squalls of wind and rain, low visibility, and ice in the vicinity, some support was welcome. Even in such conditions a field of ice can be seen or heard in good time, it is the odd floe that drifts away on its own that is a menace to a small boat. Presently we had to let draw to sail clear of a floe and soon after that started the engine to avoid another. Even this did not rouse any curiosity on the part of the crew, but at 4 a.m. when a line of ice appeared ahead we called them up to put the boat about. By breakfast time the wind had steadied to a good force six, the sea rough enough to conceal the odd floe lurking in the wave troughs. Quite suddenly we were confronted at close quarters by a cluster of floes and small bergs and in the rough water she missed stays. With little room to spare I had to gybe all standing and split the stays'l. After first making a nonsense of it the crew got the storm jib set and to my relief, after some heart-stopping moments, we were again under control. As the wind took off snow began to fall, the air temperature down to 1° C. This short-lived vicious northerly blow put me in mind of Lecky's warning that a falling barometer with a northerly wind is a signal that cannot be disregarded with impunity.

On 7th August we enjoyed for the first time what I call a 'Greenland' day, calm, cloudless, serene. For twenty miles we motored towards the land through widely scattered floes, skirting many majestic icebergs, while I sat on deck in the warm sun repairing the torn stays'l. With fog hanging low over the land we had little idea how close we were or how far south of Angmagssalik, so when the ice became thicker we retreated to more open water and lay-to for the night. A night of wind and rain gave way to a day of drizzle and the same cold, northerly wind. I felt unwell, added a third sweater, and spent the day

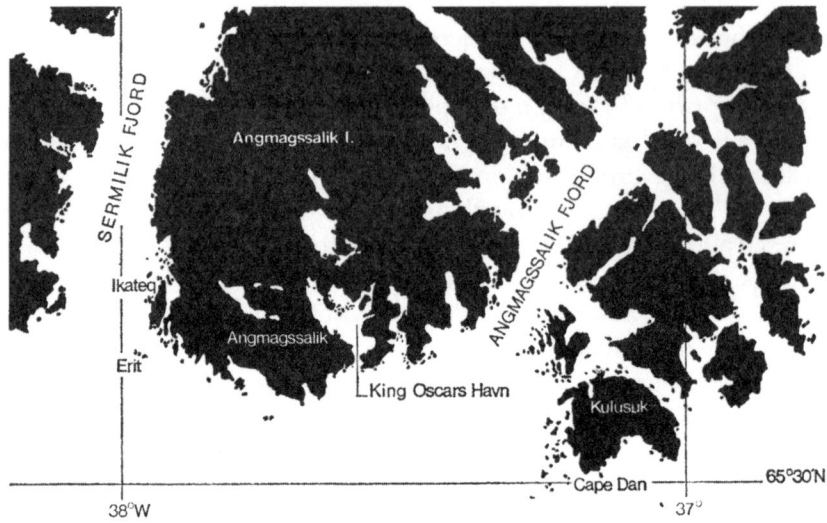

Map 5: Approaches to Angmagssalik

in my bunk, the crew standing my watches. 9th August was drier but otherwise no better; the same cold, northerly blast, drifting south, rolling damnably, knowing neither our own position nor that of the ice. However, we had the stays'l below and finished it, and if my stitches looked a bit erratic, those of Jim and Richard, plying their 'prentice hands, were frightful. We were not in a strong or even a satisfactory position. From what we had seen the ice near the coast seemed pretty thick, our bread was already finished and we had little biscuit left. We could wait for a few days but if we then failed to reach Angmagssalik we were in for a lean time. That evening the wind fell light leaving behind a nasty lop. To steady her we set all sail, pointing north-east but barely moving, with the hard, white line of the pack showing up to the north and to the west.

This waiting game would have been less trying could we but have stayed still. Unless we could keep on the move northwards we lost ground fast to the south, set down by the current. That we had lost a lot became clear next day when we motored for thirty miles in a north-westerly direction before meeting any ice. Early in the afternoon of this bright, windless day, motoring over the calmest of seas with no ice yet in sight, I had felt so confident of reaching the coast that I had the anchor got ready and hoisted our Danish courtesy flag. By 5 p.m. we were in contact with fairly close pack stretching in a wide arc from C. Dan to Sermilik fjord, close enough pack to discourage any attempt at bashing a way through. Sermilik fjord looked open and although we now had an engine that worked I felt that to enter would be courting a repetition of the 1972 disaster when we lost *Sea Breeze*. Much to the chagrin of the crew we turned about and sailed north-east, for by then a light breeze had come in.

The wind died at night, we drifted south, and at the start of yet another frustrating day we were once more south of Sermilik fjord. The ice seemed to have spread out from the coast and unlike the previous day it proved bitterly cold. To avoid the constant set to the south I thought of anchoring under Cape Tycho Brahe at the southern entrance to Sermilik fjord which at that moment looked reachable. By late afternoon I regretted we had not tried this. In thick, drizzly weather we were dodging in fairly thick ice on the north side of Sermilik, quite cut off from C. Tycho Brahe by a line of unnavigable ice. Once more we beat a retreat.

12th August, a dull, windless day, happened to be David's birthday and we nearly made it a really happy one. Having motored for three hours we entered the ice and found the going easy, so easy that I became confident of success and imparted this to David. He was at the engine controls while I stood on deck—to see better—holding the tiller line and dodging floes. There were seals about, in the sea and on the ice, and when we were within a couple of miles of Ortumuviak we spotted some seal-hunters. Ortomuviak is a bold headland only some two miles south of King Oscar's Havn, the entrance to Angmagssalik, and had we found an inshore lead we were home and dry. As it was we were stuck, the ice ahead being too thick for us to penetrate and beyond it no hint of open water. One of the seal-hunters came on board—no kayak, but a fibre-glass dory astern of which he towed a big harp seal he had just shot. Richard, who had spent some time in Norway, tried to converse in halting Danish of which our visitor understood little. He said there was open water ahead but having climbed to the crosstrees and spent some time there he seemed less confident. I took the hint and by seven o'clock we were back in ice-free water. Two more Greenlanders in a motor boat came out for a gam, one of a rather superior type, the other fulfilling one's idea of a real Eskimo, squalid, uncouth, with a perpetual amiable grin. They assured us we could not get in and would not get in next day either. This attempt, our third, had nearly succeeded. At moderate speed the engine used only ½ gal. an hour so that we had fuel enough for several more attempts. Bread was another matter and by now Jim had started to make soda-bread. I see from my diary that I was 'becoming a little browned off with all this fruitless manoeuvring in ice and shall be heartily glad to have done'.

On the 13th we enjoyed another flawless 'Greenland' day, the icebergs mirrored in the still water and beyond them a background of wild, jagged peaks. The ice in our vicinity had thickened and spread eastwards, so we used the engine to round the easternmost corner and then set sail for a light southerly breeze. On the way we met a Norwegian whaler busy seeking along the ice edge. We hoisted our ensign, waved, and made what noise we could, hoping to get some bread off him, but he ignored us and stood on. For the first time we had in sight the big radar discs on C. Dan about fifteen miles to the northwest and reckoned we were just holding our own against the current. Besides an Early Warning station there is an air-strip at C. Dan and a harbour, Kulusuk, some sixteen miles E.N.E. of Angmagssalik. The air-strip is used mostly by small charter planes from Reykjavik. That night, as well as the lights at Kulusuk, we enjoyed a moderate display of aurora. In sharp contrast we spent the next day in fog, miserably damp and chill, tacking back and forth to the ice edge. All ills are alleviated by food and since this was a Saturday the curry and duff were the more welcome.

The onset of a south-westerly breeze, the first we had had, lent encouragement, for it might well open up the ice inshore. Having noted a small tanker lying-to we closed him and after a lot of backing and filling made fast alongside. It was a Canadian tanker, *Jos Simard*, and they were waiting for the American ice-breaker *South Wind*, due at 4 a.m. next day, to assist them into Kulusuk. After Kulusuk they had three E.W.S. bases on the Baffin Island coast to supply. I had a talk with the ship's officers in their mess, all in their shirt-sleeves in that overheated room and not a uniform amongst them. It was impossible to tell who was who. The crew did better by going to the men's mess where they had a square meal. This lucky meeting solved our bread problem, for they gave us fifteen loaves, baked, I noticed, in Montreal, not by their cook. After this pleasant interlude we pushed on for our fourth attempt and were finally stopped off Ortumuviak in much the same place as before. In the evening on the way back, after getting stuck in a cul-de-sac where we took half an hour to turn round, we moored to a convenient floe, large, flat, and fitted with rudimentary bollards, with *Jos Simard* in sight a few miles away. This floe served the purpose though it was nothing like so substantial as the one we were moored to for five days in *Sea Breeze*. With ice-axes the bollards were soon improved and we were now able to stretch our legs, as it were, on shore. An ivory gull, the most beautiful of all the gulls, with pure white plumage, alighted on the floe for a short time. Jim, a keen and knowledgeable bird-watcher, identified it. I wanted to see what *Jos Simard* did. We did not want to follow in her wake—I had tried that lark in *Mischief* in '64—nor did we want to go to Kulusuk, but from it there might be a shore-lead to Angmagssalik so by watching *Jos Simard* and the ice-breaker we might discover the most likely approach. My plan miscarried. When *South Wind* arrived on time they moved off and were soon out of sight, and instead of calling me at 4 a.m. for my watch David, meaning kindly, let me lie and we remained moored to our floe.

At ten o'clock we got under way, high time, too, as the ice was on the move and thickening. Having reached open water we hoisted sail for a light breeze, steering for C. Dan off which there seemed to be little or no ice. Inside the cape the ice receded in a great bight towards Angmagssalik fjord and had it not been late evening we might have had a closer look; instead we hove-to for the night and proceeded to lose our hard-won northing. Indeed we seemed to lose more than ever. Next morning, after motoring for two hours through scattered floes, it was disheartening to find ourselves opposite C. Tycho Brahe on the south side of Sermilik fjord. However, the ice had apparently moved south. Towards Angmagssalik conditions looked much better and when we were eventually stopped I reckoned we were within a mile of Ortumuviak. Still we could see no open water close inshore while Sermilik fjord was now chock full of ice. It was late evening by then and nine o'clock before we were back in open water with all sail set for a nice south-westerly breeze. When a motor boat appeared in chase we hove-to and were presently boarded by the same Greenlander that we had met before. He had no seal in tow this time, instead he had a nice, new pair of sealskin boots. He was now confident we could get in and offered to show us the way, an offer which I accepted with some reluctance, for it would soon be dark. He headed towards the north side of Sermilik fjord at a brisk pace and only once or twice did he have to wait while we manoeuvred ourselves through some narrow passage. By midnight he had brought us into a moderately wide inshore lead a mile or two south of Ortumuviak. There he disappeared into the night leaving us to our own devices. We never saw the man again and since he would surely have looked us up in Angmagssalik, even if only to claim a reward, I think he must have come from the small settlement in Sermilik fjord.

By then it was dark, loose bits of ice hard to see, so I handed over to Richard who had keener sight. A half-moon shining directly down our course helped and if one could refrain from anxiously scanning our surroundings, a rocky shore on one side and ice on the other, immediately overhead the aurora was staging a remarkably brilliant display, bands of light, whorls, shimmering curtains, and transient flickering shafts. We passed close under Ortumuviak, the goal we had twice narrowly failed to reach, and beyond it we presently made out the faintly flashing light marking the entrance to King Oscar's Havn. On opening up the entrance we met a powerful wind blowing straight out of the fjord, and when we turned towards the entrance we had to keep the engine going hard to make headway against it. Watching the little light to starboard creep past fearfully slowly I could not forget the jostling floes and bergs to seaward of our narrow shore-lead, nor ignore the possibility of the engine failing or faltering and of our drifting back helplessly among them.

Having taken over the tiller I soon found that we could steer but in one direction, dead into the wind. The moment the bow fell off, however slightly, there was no recovering; one had to let her go right round in full circle and with gathering speed head once more into the wind. This being so we had no chance of reaching the harbour whose lights we could see away on the port hand; so we stood on for the head of the fjord hoping to find a lee under the mountains together with some sort

King Oscar's Havn, East Greenland; the peak on the right is 3500 ft.

of anchorage. As we groped our way in the dark towards the head of a small inlet, the wind already appreciably less, for a long time the leadsman reported 'no bottom'. Then suddenly five fathoms, and by the time the bunglers got the anchor over, only two. The occasional williewaw that swept down from the mountains made her drag. We had to anchor afresh and by the time we had finished it was 6 a.m. and time for breakfast—a welcome end to yet another night to remember. As I was turning in Hamish, who had the anchor watch, asked: 'Should you fall asleep do you want waking so that we can get to Angmagssalik?'

CHAPTER XV

ANGMAGSSALIK TO REYKJAVIK

THE GALE ACCOMPANIED BY RAIN went on throughout the following day. By then we had two anchors down and twice had to relay them on account of dragging. The next evening we thought the wind had moderated and discovered our mistake only when we emerged from the inlet into the main fjord. In half a mind to go back I foolishly ran on before the gale to find when we reached the harbour that it was almost blocked by ice. As we tried to creep through a small gap between a grounded floe and a Norwegian vessel lying at the quay the Norwegian chose that moment to cast off. In avoiding him we pranged the floe with our bowsprit, luckily without damage, and having backed out of the ensuing melee we anchored off a rocky shore some two cables from the harbour entrance. Our anchorage of former years, outside of and near the root of the quay, was merely a mass of ice. After more dragging, by 10 p.m., with two anchors down, we seemed at last to be fairly static. The wind had taken off and our only troubles were from drifting floes. On the whole it had been an unwise move, leaving a doubtful anchorage on a weather shore for a precarious anchorage on a lee shore with the addition of menacing floes.

The warning in the *Pilot* that has already been mentioned— 'Anchoring in this bight should be prompted by necessity and not in any hope of tranquillity'—certainly applied to our anchorage off that rocky shore, dictated by necessity and affording no tranquillity. David and I stayed on deck until 5 a.m. busy at first fending off floes and then, when the tide ebbed, relaying the anchors in order to get clear of the boulders on which she began to bump. After inspecting the ice-strewn harbour I thought we should be better off inside, and having moved inside we secured to a small local boat which we were assured would not be moving for three days. When she moved that evening we went alongside the small quay where we learnt that a small tanker would shortly arrive. Finally we found some peace at the anchorage of former

Sailing among ice in King Oscar's Havn

years whence by then most of the ice had drifted out. The harbour is small, the inner shallower half is a clutter of small boat moorings, at the one big mooring buoy there are usually two or three local boats, and at the quay itself there is room for only one vessel of any size.

After two days of wind and rain we were now enjoying the brilliant weather that I associate with Greenland, especially the east coast. The three younger crew went up what I call 'Spy-glass hill', the hill of nearly 2000 ft. that lies close behind the town, from which in 1964, when the ice had imprisoned us for three weeks, we used to scan the sea outside for possible routes of escape. In those days I used to climb it before breakfast in three quarters of an hour or less; next day when David and I thought to go up I foundered 500 ft. below the top. David, too, failed to make it, hastening down, as he said, in response to what he took to be cries for help, possibly from the skipper! This poor performance indicated to me that the wear and tear of a disheartening voyage had begun to tell on a frame no longer resilient—and worse was yet to come. Nevertheless, now that sufficient time has elapsed for the 1976 crew to become merely a distasteful memory, I am thankful to report that the Welsh equivalent of Spy-glass Hill is again well within compass. Thanks to rest, coupled with a diet of home-brewed beer, home-made bread, cheese, honey, and apple dumplings, spurred on, too, by my four-footed friends:—at 2000 ft. I no longer succumb to mountaineer's foot, the inability to put one in front of the other.

We devoted one morning to taking photographs of *Baroque* under sail in the fjord, dropping Jim, our expert photographer, in the dinghy and then making several runs past him. Next day the three young climbers set off for the peak that we had climbed in 1964. It is about 3500 ft. and they had a row of about a mile across the fjord, and a walk of three or four miles to the foot of the climb. Even so they took an unconscionable time. At four o'clock we spotted them through binoculars about half-way up but they did not get back until three o'clock next morning. Apparently they had tried a new route which failed to 'go' and in the end had to resort to the gully by which we had made the ascent. By this time I had made the rounds of Angmagssalik, meeting only one friend of 1964, Martin Petersen, the shipwright carpenter who had repaired *Mischief*'s damaged planks. He had now a fine, new workshop with power-driven saws and lathe. Martin has a little

English, unlike the few more ancient Greenlanders who recognised me with whom I could exchange only grins. Another old acquaintance, one that I regarded as slightly ominous, was the Norwegian vessel with which we had nearly collided on our first approach. She was *Brandal*, the same vessel that had tried to tow the by then much battered *Mischief* from Jan Mayen to Norway in 1968, now on charter at Angmagssalik as a sort of maid-of-all-work, hard worked at that. None of her present crew had been on board in 1968.

On 25th August, another wet day, we went alongside the quay to fill up with water and fuel for the homeward passage which was to begin the next day. I intended going north of Iceland in order to call at the island of Grimsey, thus just crossing the Arctic Circle. This crossing had become a ritual for *Baroque* which I felt could not be omitted even on this irresolute voyage. By noon a wind of almost gale force was blowing straight into the harbour and we were content to remain where we were. Had we wanted to move it had become almost impossible and at that moment my old friend *Brandal* hove in sight, back from one of her all too frequent local passages, evidently in a hurry to come alongside. A local boat moored round the corner of the quay had her stern sticking out far enough to prevent us dropping back and just off the quay was the large floe aground that had been there when we arrived and was still there when we left. And to confuse things further more floes were now drifting into the entrance. The harbourmaster (a Greenlander) soon sized up our predicament and *Brandal*'s. Summoning his gang he took charge very efficiently. Casting off the local boat they let her go down the harbour on a long warp and then paid out our warps until we could secure alongside her, whereupon *Brandal*, patiently lying-to outside, moved in to the quay.

There had been more than one black day on this voyage and the next day, 26th August, proved blackest of all. By morning there were three of us lying together on long warps from the quay, *Baroque* in the middle, and having disentangled ourselves we motored slowly towards the entrance keeping to the side opposite to the quay to avoid ice-floes. We got too near the side. In Greenland fjords it is usually safe to go within spitting distance of a rock shore but not on this occasion. We should have gone astern, instead we came firmly to rest on a rock on a falling tide. As she floated easily enough at high water that evening I might have laughed the incident off as a minor mistake; what followed this mistake was disastrous and no laughing matter at all. Having wasted some time trying vainly to kedge off I picked up the first handy coil of rope, shackled it to the throat halyard block and sent Richard ashore to anchor it. We were close to the oil installation where some concrete posts came in useful as strong points. I had thought of using this coil of rope for the mainsheet and when I tried putting in an eye-splice had found the strands so tightly laid up that I gave it best. It proved to be nylon with apparently unlimited stretch. By the time I had grasped this and begun to unreeve the peak halyards for use as a masthead line *Baroque* had listed to 45° and was beyond recovery. The nylon line went on stretching until she finished up on her beam ends, the deck vertical. Meantime David had been trying to lighten her, sending ashore the heavy anchor and cable, draining the water tanks, and even lifting the floor-boards with a view to getting out the ballast—all to no purpose.

By afternoon we had four lines from mast to shore, a tackle on each, together with a very capable Greenlander who came along to encourage and assist. With David and I tailing behind he did most of the work as we gained a few inches on each line in turn in an effort to get the boat upright before the rising tide flooded her. I never saw the rest of the crew who must have gone shopping. At the extreme angle the boat lay over, the lines had little lifting power and needless to say the tide won, rising inexorably inch by inch, until long before we had her even half upright she was completely full of water. Little enough that was of use or value had been got out—all the food, except that in tins, was destroyed, clocks, barometer, binoculars, camera, film, radio, clothes, sleeping bags, and worst of all the engine and batteries, all soaked in a mixture of diesel oil and sea water. A number of Danes and Greenlanders had gathered on the rocks to watch. One of the Green-landers took the opportunity to pocket a thousand or so of David's cigarettes lying among the small pile of stuff that had been salvaged. When detected by David and forced to disgorge the bystanders merely laughed, evidently more in sympathy with the culprit than with his victim. Among the Danes was the man in charge of the oil installation who offered at a price, a high one, to pump out the boat. They ran a power line down, put a pump on board, and within an hour had all the water out. By then she had floated off so I got them to tow her to the buoy. We then began ferrying the salvaged stuff on board in the dinghy. I stood by until the last load had gone and it was about 10 p.m. before I got back on board.

What a homecoming! Anything floatable had floated so that debris lay about everywhere, a film of oil covered everything, the floorboards were up, and both pumps were at work. While lying on her beam ends a plank had been started. David slightly lessened the copious flow by cutting up a rag and stuffing bits in, but the pumps had to be kept going all night. A hut at the oil installation had kindly been put at our disposal and we took it in turns to row over and doss down for a couple of hours in a warm, dry room. Early in the morning I got hold of Martin who came off and speedily stopped the leak with his sawdust trick. A bucketful of sawdust with a long pole attached to the handle is capsized alongside bottom up, thrust smartly down to the vicinity of the leak where, by joggling the pole, the sawdust escapes and is sucked into the leak. A refinement is to have a box with a sliding lid, actuated by a line, fixed to the pole. When the box is in position the lid is drawn and the sawdust released. I arranged with Martin that after the week-end we would beach *Baroque* so that he could put tingles over the leak.

David and Jim had drained the engine and cleaned it out but the electrical parts needed professional attention. Through the hospital doctor, whom I knew, I got in touch with a Dane who ran a taxi and plant-hire business who sent two of his mechanics on board that evening. They soon had the cylinder off and took the batteries, dynamo, and starter motor to their workshop. From the doctor, by the way, we received other kindnesses including gifts of whale meat and arctic char and the use of his house to dry out our gear. Our beaching arrangements looked like being in jeopardy when the local hospital ship limped in with propeller trouble. The beach, which is reasonably smooth, is very small and the hospital ship obviously had first claim; in the end, however, Martin, who is in charge of all repair work, got us in together. The acting skipper of the hospital ship paid me a visit along with his cook, also acting, who turned out to be an Englishman, a very dark one. The skipper's real motive was to buy spirits and I had to tell him I would rather he drank them on board, which he did with a will. Greenlanders can buy alcohol only in the form of beer (Carlsberg or

Tuborg lager) and the sale of that is stopped on Fridays in the hope that the wives will be able to grab enough of their man's wages for housekeeping. The skipper looked forward to retiring early in order to devote all his time to the business or pastime of seal-hunting to which he was addicted. His English was nearly as good as that of the cook and both became increasingly voluble. Not surprisingly, from this rum session only one item of seal lore remains clear, namely that the blue-back skin is the best, followed by that of the ring seal.

Except for David the crew had now taken to sleeping ashore. The boat seemed the more wholesome for it though I realised that it would be difficult to sail without them. They turned up on the Monday and at high water we rowed the boat with our sweeps on to the beach in the wake of the hospital ship. The rise and fall of the tide is from eight to ten feet and in the absence of any wall to lean against we rigged lines to keep her upright. By late evening Martin had finished his tingles of felt covered with aluminium sheet and we kedged off as soon as she floated. Instead of the calm conditions of the morning there were violent gusts of wind and what with this and the numerous small craft yawing wildly at their moorings we had to anchor before we were in deep enough water. By midnight, with another three hours of ebb to go, she was on the bottom. With the sweeps and a big baulk of timber David and I rigged legs and also took a long line from the mast ashore. Half of this long line turned out to be the same damned line that had literally let us down before, but the boat was still upright and every ten minutes or so we took in the slack by hauling on the throat halyards. The legs appeared to be taking most of the weight so when the mast line became block on block we let it go in order to shorten it, where-upon the lashing of the midships leg parted and over she went with a bang. She was nothing like right over and by pumping we kept the water down until she began to lift when, having rigged another mast-head line, by heaving in on both we presently got her upright. David and I spent the night on deck, the crew's contribution being pumping and saving their gear from the threatened inundation.

My relations with them were becoming strained and these came to a head the next afternoon. After our all-night performance I wanted some sleep and with Richard prowling about on deck in his climbing boots I found it difficult. My suggestion that he should either come below or jump over the side was not well received. All three hastened below to announce that they were quitting, that they were unhappy, and that the boat was not safe. What, I think, they really wanted was to oblige me to leave the boat at Angmagssalik and so make me responsible for getting them home. Rather than this I reckoned that David and I could take her to Reykjavik and hope to get some more crew there. Richard took his gear ashore, Hamish packed his but continued using the boat as a restaurant, while Jim, who had some sense of duty, declared that 'he was ready to stick his neck out' but only as far as Reykjavik, and always provided the engine worked.

Owing to the exertions of the last few days I felt extremely weak and could only crawl around. We had once more to arrange for taking on water and fuel and before that could be done the fuel tanks needed draining off and a water pipe had to be repaired. When she was full of water the cabin water tank had come adrift and broken the outlet pipe. At this time *Tycho Brahe* came in. She had landed her geologists at Kulusuk, whence they would fly home, and she was now homeward bound empty. Her skipper, whom I did not meet, apparently advised or even invited *Baroque*'s crew to take passage with him. Richard was on board like a shot and that night, or rather at three in the morning, a voice by my bunk was heard intoning: 'This is Hamish. I've come to tell you that I'm leaving.'

In the morning (4th Sept.) we warped up to the quay astern of *Tycho Brahe* who was supposed to be leaving. Her skipper must have been of a cautious disposition for though she was a vessel built to shunt ice, and by then there was little enough left to shunt, he was waiting for a helicopter report on ice conditions. She finally got away, spurred on by *Brandal* which was again waiting to come in, with Richard and Hamish safely on board, Richard on deck busy with warps, Hamish out of sight below. On reflection I believe that *Tycho Brahe* did me a good rather than an ill turn. Without her Richard and Hamish looked like being marooned and the Danish authorities in Greenland dislike having on their hands penniless foreigners. I should have had to tell the local Governor that I was leaving behind two of my crew and he would no doubt have taken the line that since I had brought them there I should have to get them away, or in other words have them flown to Reykjavik. Some moderately kind words are no doubt owing to Jim, who all along had been apprehensive, for resisting the terrible temptation offered by *Tycho Brahe*, especially as the engine had not yet been started and might well never start. That was settled the same evening when the two mechanics came and in a short time had it running as well as ever. As there would no doubt still be some ice outside to negotiate this was a great relief.

After the severe strains we had recently put upon the mast the shrouds needed setting up again and also the forestay. David stripped down the water-logged barometer and finally got it to work. The ship's clock, the chronometer watch, and the wireless set were all too badly corroded, as well as my camera. Except for the clock which looks well when polished even if it does not go, I dropped them all overboard. David's quartz clock still functioned. I had intended sailing on 6th Sept. but by the time the bill for the engine repairs—a hefty one—had been settled we had not enough time left to get clear of the ice before dark. When we left early the next morning, the water in the harbour and in King Oscar's Havn was covered with cat-ice. A field of fairly close pack extended from the entrance to C. Dan but south of this there were only a few scattered floes and a great many bergs. By 6 p.m., after motoring all day, we were in ice-free water. Feeling greatly in need of a quiet sea voyage after the harrowing experiences of the past fortnight I had reason to be thankful. Storms, ice, and the damage they can do are acceptable as part of the game, but damage inflicted by one's own mistakes is more painful, less easily borne, and not readily forgotten.

The first three days of this short passage were calm, cloudless, and without a breath of wind. We motored more or less non-stop and when I insisted on stopping the engine for the sake of having four hours of quiet in the middle of the night, the other two regarded me as no better than a 'cissy'. On the fourth day we had all the wind we wanted and eventually hove-to with six rolls in the mains'l. She was leaking rather more than usual, a circumstance that might put a severe strain on Jim's fragile loyalty. In the morning, however, I discovered the source of this additional leak close to the head of my bunk and just above the water line. Every roll of the boat produced a miniature water-spout. Putting her about so that she heeled the right way, we hove-to while David tacked on a tingle of canvas, putty, and aluminium sheet. With Jim holding on to his feet he could just reach down far enough.

With no latitude sight the previous day, on the sixth day out we found we were heading for Snaefell (4759 ft.), the snow-capped mountain on the northern side of the wide Faxafloi bight. Mindful of the liberal error of our first landfall I had allowed too much for the vagaries of the compass, and besides that a strong north-going current sets up the west coast of Iceland. As we closed the land a fog-bank drifted in from seawards reducing visibility to barely a cable's length. An hour later it cleared with remarkable suddenness revealing, close on our port hand, the snowy dome of Snaefell glistening in the setting sun. We made Reykjavik next day, a week out from Angmagssalik, again securing to the floating crane. On this passage we did a lot more motoring than sailing, for since David and Jim had to all the hoisting and changing of sails I was loth to call them up too often.

In the course of their long, fruitful collaboration over the recent engine problems they had become pretty matey and David now confided to me that the apprehensive Jim, if treated gently, would probably remain with us all the way home. This he finally agreed to do provided I would land him at his home-town Fort William or at worst Oban. Looking back it occurs to me that from quite early on democrat Jim had more or less dictated the course of this troubled voyage; he was by no means indispensable but apart from his steady if unflamboyant work in the galley he knew more about the engine than David, and being of slight build had less difficulty in reaching its more inaccessible parts. We needed now only one or two more hands in order to complete the last leg of the voyage. The weather seemed set fair and a fine, warm spell, unusual for Iceland, continued until we were just about to sail.

As the Bulgars say, you can go nowhere, not even to church, without cash. Not surprisingly I was now short of it and accordingly called on my friend Mr. Holt at the Embassy. Aware of my crew problem he gave me the name of a friend of his who might help, a Mr. Stefanson, a keen dinghy sailor and president of some local sailing association. After much telephoning Mr. Stefanson found a man who although about to leave on holiday for Majorca professed a liking for sailing to England instead. He promised to visit *Baroque* that evening and needless to say failed to turn up. Without wishing to asperse them I must say I did find some Icelanders more prompt in their promises than in their performance, though it may well be that this applied only in such matters as shipping in *Baroque*. We had already made our wants known at the Youth Hostel and the next day Nicholas appeared, an American in his early thirties, looking and behaving, I thought, not unlike the stoical Red Indian. He did not enlarge on his past, we gathered only that he had some knowledge of computers and being anxious to forget it had taken to travel. He had a flight to Luxembourg next day, thence to Munich for some festival, and later to Nepal. He had no sea experience whatever but confessed to cooking and since he seemed keener on sailing to England than flying to Luxembourg I took him on. He brought his traps on board next day, having cancelled his flight, and also brought a Norwegian friend, John, who wanted to come. He had no sea experience either and a more unlikely looking sailor would be hard to find—lanky, bespectacled, flaxen hair down to his shoulders, and a beard. Nevertheless, in the very short time these two were with us one could see that John had in him the makings of a useful hand while Nicholas seemed to have no aptitude. John spoke a little English and both were inveterate smokers, rolling their own cigarettes. With these two and the two remaining original hands—if Nicholas took on the galley—I felt we could manage all right and fixed sailing day for 18th Sept. On the 16th the weather broke, raining and blowing hard from south-east, the direction from which Iceland gets most of its wind and rain since most depressions pass to the south. Short-handed though we were then, had we but sailed from Angmagssalik direct for the U.K., by the time the fine spell broke we should have been on the south side of the depressions and enjoying westerly winds.

On the 18th it was still blowing hard from the same hostile quarter and that afternoon I walked out to the Meteorological Office to learn what the prospects were. A big low to the south was almost stationary, nor would the weather men promise anything better than south-easterlies force six to seven for the next day or two. After three days of wet weather with nothing to do we were all restive and anxious to be off. Weather forecasts have been known to be wrong, and although I had a graveyard cough and a sore throat I decided to sail the next day, a Sunday. As a reward for this impatience it may be said that I deserved all that followed but those who say so should try lying alongside a crane in Reykjavik harbour for four wet and windy days.

Sheltered by the land we sailed down the coast in relatively calm conditions until we began to open up the strait between Reykjanes and Eldey rock where we met the full force of the south-easterly. We were under stays'l and trys'l and even with the mains'l set, to beat through the strait in the teeth of a near gale would have been a thankless task. We kept her pointing west of south, thankful to have Eldey rock and its thirty-mile-long reef to windward. With the rock still in sight and darkness falling we were about to have supper when the head of the stays'l blew out. Supper had to wait until we had both sails down and were lying a-hull, losing ground steadily to the west. The most astonishing thing about this rough start was how the landsmen Nicholas and John reacted. They failed to react at all. Neither showed any qualms of sea-sickness or uneasiness and carried on unconcernedly rolling endless cigarettes and eating their meals. Wind and rain continued all night and although the man on watch could shelter in the lee of the doghouse or inside I was thankful when David offered to take my watch. We lay-to all next day in the same disagreeable weather while I had the stays'l sent below and put in the morning stitching. Apart from that I lay at earth, missing meals, and thus remained ignorant of the consultations that were no doubt going on and unprepared for the impending 'bombshell', the name that journalists have for the unexpected.

Though still in the same quarter, by morning the wind had moderated and I was feeling more like myself. It was time to start sailing. Whereupon Jim piped up with a demand that we return to Reykjavik and to my astonishment and dismay David, who hitherto had been a tower of strength, doing his utmost for the success of the voyage, backed him up. 'Et tu Brute,' was my inevitable thought as he gave his reasons—the boat leaking, a new suit of sails needed, the skipper on the point of collapse, and another depression imminent. Naturally our two landsmen took no part in the heated dispute that followed, and considering their indifference to the weather of the last two days they must have wondered what all the fuss was about, that the two whom they took to be hardened sailors, accustomed to gales, should want to turn back. With David's support we could have taken the unhappy Jim home willy-nilly, but with the two of them bent on going back there was nothing to be done.

Besides the folly of ever spending a day or half a day in one's bunk, this episode brought home to me another disadvantage that this particular bunk had in addition to its proximity to the galley and the heads, its poor light, and a certain amount of dampness, namely that of being apart from and out of touch with the crew; so that even if one, as it were, smelt a rat, one could not, to continue the metaphor, nip it in the bud. This forced return to Reykjavik had enough implications, I think, to preclude its being received with good grace. A winter in Iceland, hauled out for something like seven months, would not improve *Baroque*, and it put paid to any lingering hopes I may have had of a voyage the following year. While Reykjavik is well placed geographically for a northern voyage, fitting out and the buying of stores there would be prohibitively expensive, and to that would be added the cost of flying out a crew.

David's imminent depression turned into an anti-cyclone that for the next week embraced Iceland and the surrounding waters. We sailed back in benign weather, sweetness and light everywhere except in *Baroque*, and by the time we made fast alongside our too familiar crane I had the stays'l repaired. Next morning Stefan, surprised by our return, took me out to Jon Elevan's yard where I made arrangements for the boat's wintering. She could not be hauled out at once as Jon had to get his slipway ready and a cradle built. He had a respect for old wooden boats, felt as much concern for *Baroque* as I did, and I was confident she would be in good hands. On returning I found David alone, Jim having already taken his gear ashore. For some reason he had undergone a change of mind and heart. I had misunderstood him and jumped to conclusions; his sole concern had been for my health and he was quite willing to finish the voyage.

Anxious as ever to get the boat home I took this revised version at its face value. As the Arabs say, the camel driver has his thoughts and the camel he has his, so I set about the unpromising task of finding a replacement for Jim. He had to be a man with some sailing experience, for we could not cope with three landsmen, and he had to be quickly available, for the season was well advanced. Having warned Jon Elevan that we might yet get away I gave myself until the next Sunday, 26th Sept., to find him. My friend Mr. Stefanson seemed hopeful. He had two men in view and they promised to see me that evening. The one who turned up said he could not get away but he had strong hopes that Specky, as he was known, who had failed to come, would be a likely starter. On my reporting progress or the lack of it to Mr. Stefanson he gave poor Specky a telephone lecture on the need for keeping appointments and got from him a firm promise to turn up next day at 4 p.m. Even so I was not much surprised when at the appointed hour Mr. Stefanson himself came on board to say that Specky had cried off. Our last hope was now the Fishermen's Union many of whose members apparently took a holiday at this time of year, generally in Majorca. *Baroque* could not compete with Majorca, for although for many Icelanders the sea is their livelihood we never found one who wanted to make it his playground.

On the Monday, therefore, we unbent the sails, unshipped the bowsprit, and unrove the running rigging, stripping her to a gantline as the saying goes. In the absence of anyone else able or willing the skipper, despite his recently alleged failing health, spent an hour or so aloft unshackling and sending down all the wire ropes, blocks, and strops. When the gear had been labelled Jon took it to his store. Nicholas and John were still on board to give us a hand, and apart from my own feelings over this mournful affair I felt that they had been badly let down. In due course, I hope *Baroque* will sail back to England and that will probably be my last voyage in her. As my birthday is in February it would be difficult to celebrate my eightieth north of the Arctic Circle, though I should have liked to have made a voyage in her in 1978 if only as a gesture of defiance. However, steeply rising costs and waning strength had already inclined me to call a halt, and now with the boat lying at Reykjavik, together with the frightening possibility that one might again be stuck with a similar crew, the decision is no longer in doubt. As Conrad's old seaman Singleton remarked: 'Ships are all right, it's the men in them.'

The verses below by Humbert Wolfe are by way of farewell to the few who have followed my varied fortunes. They appeal especially to me now because three great beech trees below the window where I write are still stripping themselves. In the last verse perhaps poetic license will allow the use of 'running close-hauled' though it grates on a seaman's ear. Just as it is proverbially impossible to blow and swallow at the same time, so is it to run and sail close-hauled.

Listen! The wind is rising
and the air is wild with leaves;
we have had our summer evenings;
now for October eves.

The great beech trees lean forward,
and strip like a diver, we
had better turn to the fire
and shut our mind to the sea

where the ships of youth are running
close-hauled on the edge of the wind,
with all adventure before them
and only the old behind.

Bodowen
November 1976

Afterword

Bob Comlay

EXPLORING THE RELATIONSHIP between H.W. Tilman and his crew members can help to shed light on the compassionate side of his character, a trait that the popular yachting press has often found convenient to ignore.

At home with his sister Adeline, in the company of his niece Pam, or aboard ship with a good crew when things were going well, Tilman's impeccably timed and mischievous wit kept spirits high, the humour as often as not turned on himself. In unfamiliar surroundings however, his natural reticence could easily be misinterpreted by those who had not had the privilege of personal acquaintance. One high profile yachting journalist, cultivating the popular curmudgeonly image of his subject, wrote that 'of all the crews who ever sailed with Tilman, only one man ever repeated the experience'. Had he read more widely, he would have found that there were no fewer than nine crew-members who returned for a second voyage, one of them, 'even more eccentric', making four. There would have been others but for the difficulty of taking extended periods of unpaid leave from employment.

Many of Tilman's crew members remained in contact with him after their voyages had ended and several have come forward with stories of the Skipper's concern for their wellbeing. Bruce Reid, Tilman's climbing partner for the crossing of Bylot Island in 1963, had been destined for the RAF after leaving *Mischief*. Tragically, it was to be a career cut short by a flying accident which left him wheelchair-bound. He spoke to me recently of his surprise when Tilman visited him in recovery at Stoke Mandeville hospital, and to this day he is still grateful for the support and encouragement that the Skipper gave him.

In later years, Tilman's increasingly young crew members could be divided into two categories: those who were already aware of the man and his travels before they signed up and those who had little or no idea what they were actually letting themselves in for. In December 1969 I fell firmly into the latter category. At the age of seventeen I had already secured a university place for the following year and was biding my time at school pursuing a completely unnecessary maths qualification. The discovery of Tilman's advertisement for crew was timely; the limited experience of sailing I'd had at school had left me wanting for more.

In response to my initial inquiry he wrote: 'I shall certainly consider you as a possible but cannot give you a definite answer until I've talked to you or until I know whether I'm going to get any better volunteers.' We arranged to meet at Lymington in early February aboard the pilot cutter *Sea Breeze*, built in 1899 and just a year younger than her owner. Writing later of that first encounter, Tilman described me as 'young, slightly built—not likely to break a rope by heaving on it'. My own first impression of him had similarities and I was taken aback by both the age of the man and his stature, which if anything was smaller than me. Few words passed between us, but I soon got stuck into a couple of jobs that needed sorting out which led to a later observation that I was 'never backward in making suggestions, a few of which, annoyingly enough, turned out to be right.'

Shortly afterwards, I received a letter with a reasonable set of conditions for taking me on: 'After thinking it over I have decided to offer you a berth in *Sea Breeze* if you still want to come. Admittedly you have no particular qualifications or very much experience, but that will not matter provided you pull your weight and take things as they come, the rough with the smooth. I hope I've guessed right.' It was only after we had both given our word that I walked into the reference section of my local public library, looked up 'H W Tilman' in a copy of *Who's Who*, returned home with copies of *Mischief in Patagonia* and *Mischief in Greenland* and started reading Tilman for the first time.

The 1970 voyage was summed up by Tilman as 'one of the happiest, if not the most successful. With as good a crowd a few years earlier who knows but that something of note might have been accomplished.' We may not have achieved the original climbing objectives for the trip, but spending the best part of a week beset in the Greenland pack ice had become an unexpected and unlikely high point to a happy voyage.

He wrote in a letter to me that December, 'I gave the Royal Thames YC the benefit of our experiences and it was certainly something new for them.'

We had returned to the UK already late for my first term at university, and like many of Tilman's younger crew members I found the transition to life ashore difficult. While I enjoyed the company of my new peers at Bangor, and the location if not the weather, nothing ashore could match the experience of that Arctic summer. The course on which I'd enrolled held little interest for me and my level of concentration never really stepped up into second gear. With the Skipper living close at hand in Barmouth, plans for 1971 were never far from my thoughts. I would hitch-hike down through Snowdonia to Barmouth and join him for lunch at Bodowen, the house he shared with his sister on the Mawddach Estuary. Over a lunch of his home-baked bread, his excellent home-brewed ale and a strong cheddar, we shared stories and photographs from the voyage and pondered future plans. A stroll up the hill behind the house with Bella and Toff, the dogs, would round out the afternoon before I hit the road back to Bangor. In a letter on December 15th, he wrote 'If you hear of any candidates let me know. You said you yourself might be able to come which would, of course, be fine. There's nothing like having at least one reliable chap on board.' I needed little further encouragement, drifting through the remainder of my first year and slipping out part way through my last exam paper in order to make a 'pier head jump' onto the boat at Lymington.

Our destination in 1971 was Scoresby Sound, high on the East Coast of Greenland, the largest and longest fjord system in the world, with two mountainous islands at its head, the peaks of which were still mostly unclimbed. Once again, bad ice conditions were to be our downfall and we could barely get within sight of Kap Brewster at the southern entrance to the fjord. 'Here were no scattered floes, but close, heavy polar ice, an uncompromising barrier that offered no temptation to start probing, an obstacle from which one could retreat with a clear conscience.' Despite the lack of achievement of the goal, it was another enjoyable trip, with landfalls in the Faroes, Iceland and further south on the east coast of Greenland.

On our arrival in Reykjavik, I had picked up a letter from the university informing me that unless I returned in early September to re-take the inevitably failed maths paper, my university career was over. The Skipper's immediate reaction was to offer to write to Sir Charles Evans, Principal of University College, Bangor and veteran of Everest 1953. I declined that offer but, once back in the UK, called on Sir Charles to plead on my own behalf. Evans, to my discomfort crippled with multiple sclerosis, made short work of throwing out my excuses and I felt in no position to protest further. He made it abundantly clear that while he viewed travelling with Tilman once as justifiable, repeating the experience simply demonstrated a distinct lack of commitment to an academic career. I sensed understandable bitterness that Tilman, twenty years his senior, was still engaged in such pursuits while Evans was left wrestling with Welsh university politics from the confines of a wheelchair. It was a brief meeting, I felt all the more guilty for having troubled him, thanked him for his advice and quietly withdrew.

Tilman had become an unexpected role model for me and his expedition lifestyle had become my only real 'career' aspiration. My second attempt at starting my university career was soon in tatters and for much of the winter of 1971–72, I was seriously considering dropping out and signing up for a third trip. It was with great reluctance, bolstered by parental pressure and with a belated nod to the advice of Sir Charles that I decided to give priority to the completion of my university studies. The Skipper was supportive, even if he didn't hide an attempt to play on my loyalty. 'No need to feel sore about missing a voyage this year; there will be other opportunities, if not in *Sea Breeze* then in some other ship. Father, too, will be delighted and it's always a good thing to please fathers. From my selfish point of view, it's bad. There's nothing like having someone on board who knows the ropes and someone upon whom I could rely to any extent as I could upon you.' Instead, I spent a miserable summer working in a warehouse, a state made all the more miserable by the shock news that *Sea Breeze* had foundered off the East Greenland coast. Colin Putt and I met the crew at London's Heathrow Airport on their return from Reykjavik on a commercial flight, Tilman still dressed in the carpet slippers he'd been wearing when the ship was lost. I think that Colin and I both felt some sense of responsibility for the loss of the boat, feeling that had we been aboard with our hard-won experience of her temperamental engine, the outcome might have been different.

I was not the only former crew member to fail to settle down to a 'normal' lifestyle after the experience of a voyage with Tilman. In a letter in December 1972, he wrote, 'I heard at the Arctic Club dinner from my St Andrews professor that Andrew Harwich had failed his exams and been pushed out. I had better stop taking students.'

Despite my best efforts, my inability to focus on the academic objective led to another dismal performance in a maths examination. This time, I was out for good, a back injury from the summer warehouse job rendering me incapable of travelling to Bangor to re-sit the offending examination paper. I gave up the prospect of university and, returning to fitness in the autumn, took up employment with IBM near Portsmouth. This was not to last. After a few months of sheer boredom, I pleaded with my old university tutor to be allowed to re-sit my entire first year examination set as an external candidate. Tilman, still keeping an eye on my erratic course through academic life, offered some blunt encouragement: 'I don't know whether to admire or regret your persistence at having another go at university exams. Anyhow, the best of British luck and I think you stand a good chance since apart from your hard-won experience of exams, I gather that competition for university places is markedly less and that some universities are scratching around for students.'

Confounding all the odds, I passed my first year at the third attempt and making up for lost time, finally graduated in 1975. The last two academic years passed uneventfully. My original peer community had already graduated and this time around I fell in with a rather more mature crowd. The Skipper and I kept in touch and still enjoyed Bodowen beer during winter conversations, but now I was able to exchange the hitch-hiking mode of transport, never easy in North Wales, for the loan of a left hand drive VW Beetle from a Danish post-graduate student.

In 1974, after returning from the successful but incident-packed circumnavigation of Spitzbergen, Tilman wrote, 'My sister died very suddenly in September. I knew nothing until Sandy met us coming up the river. A hard blow and a sad homecoming. Am staying here for the moment. Like the politicians, I am at a loss what to do.'

In the run up to my final exams, I kept my head down and free from distraction. Tilman's response to the news that I'd finally got myself settled in a permanent job was typically philosophical: 'I'm glad to hear that you graduated with honours and are safely ensconced in a job earning some cash. At one time, I feared you were on the way to becoming a professional student... Few of those who come with me seem to have the bottom to settle down to a job and I begin to think that I do more harm than good. However, that does not stop me and I hope to go north this summer and am in the unusual position of having a full crew and one or two spares. I think this will be the last. The expense is becoming beyond all reason, apart from my own increasing decrepitude.'

Writing after the 1976 voyage, it was clear that his premonition had been well founded; the voyage had been a disaster. 'We had an unfortunate voyage this summer. Boat and crew trouble from start to finish and ending with the crew obliging me to leave the boat at Reykjavik. I hope to bring her back next May and that will be my last voyage in her. She is too expensive to keep going, I am too old, and this year's experience was really a sickener. I have not yet faced up to the problem of what I shall do with myself, beyond growing old gracefully.'

I spent the latter part of 1976 and the spring of 1977 commuting back and forth between Southampton and Portsmouth over the Itchen Bridge, close by the site where another former Tilman crew member, Simon Richardson, was busy working on modifications to *En Avant*, his old steel tugboat hull, for an expedition to Smith Island in the Antarctic. Simon was casting around for crew for his proposed voyage and Sandy Lee had put us in touch. The meeting sounded a few warning bells, not the least of which related to the scale and viability of the conversion work being carried out on an unlikely hull. While we were both the same age, our attitudes to risk and reality were quite different; I'd already made two voyages north, struggled with university and had finally got my life back on an even keel while Simon still had the romance of high latitude adventure uppermost in his mind. The final insurmountable sticking point was the amount of cash that Simon required prospective crew members to contribute. I had forgotten the actual amount until recent conversations with John Shipton and Andrew Craig Bennett, both of whom were also approached back in 1976, reminded me that we were each expected to come up with £500. Whatever the amount, it was well beyond my means at the time and

what might have been a difficult decision—sail south or get married—
became altogether easier.

At the time of my brief discussion with Simon on the dockside in
Southampton, I had no idea that Tilman had any intention of joining
En Avant. If the idea had already been mooted, it was certainly kept in
confidence by both of them and I remained unaware of the fact until
Sandy sent me a cutting from the Southampton *Evening Echo* regard-
ing the disappearance of the ship.

I moved on and settled down to the next thirty-five years of married and corporate life. Speaking of the Skipper, Jonno Barrett, who
sailed with Tilman and Richardson on the first *Baroque* voyage, may
have hit the nail on the head: 'I often think that the true challenge was
all the stuff he avoided all his life, family, kids and what not.' Looking
back on my own life and its challenges, I'm inclined to agree. I do,
however, acknowledge the important part that Tilman played as a distant role model for those challenges and like to think that part of his
character rubbed off. In business life, as in climbing and sailing, small
efficient teams work best. Plan on the back of an envelope, lead by
example and set simple objectives: 'Take the rough with the smooth'.

H. W. TILMAN

The Collected Edition

FOR THE FIRST TIME SINCE THEIR ORIGINAL APPEARANCE, all fifteen books by H. W. Tilman are being published as single volumes, with all their original photographs, maps and charts. Forewords and afterwords by those who knew him, or who can bring their own experience and knowledge to bear, complement his own understated writing to give us a fuller picture of the man and his achievements. A sixteenth volume is the 1980 biography by J. R. L. Anderson, *High Mountains and Cold Seas*. The books will appear in pairs, one each from his climbing and sailing eras, in order of original publication, at quarterly intervals from September 2015:

Sep 2015	Snow on the Equator
	Mischief in Patagonia
Dec 2015	The Ascent of Nanda Devi
	Mischief Among the Penguins
Mar 2016	When Men & Mountains Meet
	Mischief in Greenland
Jun 2016	Mount Everest 1938
	Mostly Mischief
Sep 2016	Two Mountains and a River
	Mischief Goes South
Jan 2017	China to Chitral
	In Mischief's Wake
Apr 2017	Nepal Himalaya
	Ice With Everything
Sep 2017	Triumph and Tribulation
	High Mountains and Cold Seas

www.tilmanbooks.com